ARNA

THE JOURNAL OF THE UNIVERSITY OF SYDNEY ARTS STUDENT SOCIETY

2010

First published 2010 by Darlington Press
Darlington Press is an imprint of SYDNEY UNIVERSITY PRESS
sydney.edu.au/sup

Funded by The University of Sydney Union and The University of Sydney
Faculty of Arts

ISBN: 978-1-921364-11-2

Fisher Library F03
University of Sydney
NSW 2006 Australia
Email: sup.info@sydney.edu.au

CREDITS

Editors-in-Chief
Julian Larnach
Paul Ellis

Copy Editors
Shaun Crowe
Richard Withers

Launch Coordinators
Rachel Molden
Sarah Nguyen

Publication Manager
Alistair Stephenson

Editor, Fiction
Dominic McNeill

Editor, Essays
Rebecca Simpson

Editors, Poetry
Jess Stirling
Symonne Torpey

THANKS TO

The University of Sydney Union
The University of Sydney Faculty of Arts
The Sydney Arts Students Society
Contributors

CONTENTS

FOREWORD

Julian Larnach

———

Do not be fooled, if we write we are writers. Simple as that. Our styles, purposes and viewpoints may be different but we are all writers. We do not need qualifications, we simply need a story to tell.

I like reading. I like writing. The job of Editor-in-Chief seemed like a good combination of both. Within a few weeks, my fellow editor Paul and I, quickly shaped our vision for ARNA. We did not feel a theme was necessary as this would restrict submissions. We wanted to visit subject areas often overlooked in university literary journals, such as politics and film. We wanted a journal that would reflect the modern Arts student – eclectic and hard to pinpoint.

I'd like to thank a few people. To every contributor (successful and unsuccessful), you made our job all the more difficult – but a good kind of difficult, like opening a tricky jar and the uncertain pop of satisfaction. To the Executive of the Sydney Arts Students Society, you were constantly helpful with any request. To former editors Nancy and Callie, your experience was invaluable with matters meddlesome. To readers (once potential, now actual), you have made our job worthwhile.

Enjoy these writers as they guide you through well-constructed arguments, up and down spiritual and emotional conundrums and around worlds: magnificent and horrible.

———

THE BEAUTY
OF JACQUES
RIVETTE

Ivan Čerečina

———

Throughout his career, Jacques Rivette has remained an anomalous figure. He is one who has been difficult to categorise within the context of the French New Wave and in the broader context of postwar auteur cinema. While his work has not been without its champions, those who have been willing to fully explore the cinematic world that he has forged over the years have been few and far between. One could argue that one of the reasons for Rivette's uneasy standing in the eyes of cinema-goers has been his uniquely experimental approach to narrative which has manifested itself in a body of work that is as diverse in its scope as it is in its approach to the cinematic art itself. Though non-traditional narrative structures have been a central preoccupation of Rivette's films, it is in his early films that this approach is the most radical and effective. This essay will focus on two films from this early period, namely *Céline et Julie vont en bateau: Phantom Ladies Over Paris* (1974) and *Paris nous appartient* (1960). These films demonstrate the fundamental importance of narrative structure to the creation of meaning in Rivette's work while also showing the extent of his flexibility with narrative forms.

In an introduction to an interview with Rivette conducted in the mid-70s,

———

film critic Jonathan Rosenbaum made the following observation about the director's films up to that point:

> Every Rivette film has its Eisenstein/Lang/Hitchcock side – an impulse to design and plot, dominate and control – and its Renoir/Hawks/Rossellini side: an impulse to "let things go," open one's self up to the play and power of other personalities, and watch what happens.

Rivette frames Céline and Julie so that they become "viewers" just as we are. They are watching the play seated on a couch, commenting on it (Julie: "Oh, I've seen this bit before!") in much the same way that we are doing with the film itself. Yet, Céline and Julie are viewers who are "miraculously given the power to intervene in the action and change its predetermined course". Thus, they later go into the house and change the ending of the play by literally inserting themselves as characters and improvising action and dialogue to their advantage. By presenting us with an "audience" which is non-passive and in fact quite active in their role of viewing, Rivette is proposing an alternate way of viewing films or rather an alternate conception of the viewer's role in watch films. The audience are creators who are as vital to the final realisation of the film as the auteur himself.

Undeniably, the way in which the two female protagonists subvert the narrative form of the play in the house has resulted in *Céline et Julie* being considered one of the key feminist texts to come out of the 1970s. It has even been interpreted as bearing a lesbian-feminist polemic. The two eponymous protagonists of the film are portrayed as subversive, autonomous women who are able to successfully throw off the shackles of patriarchy, finally allowing themselves to be free and "go boating" at the end of the film. In the film, traditional narrative forms and male dominance are analogous as is demonstrated in the "house of fiction". The two women inside are "governed entirely by the inherited assumptions of patriarchy" as their lives revolve solely around trying to win over Olivier (the widower) as their husband. The women are trapped in the house by narrative forces. They appear to be forever doomed to live out the rest of their lives playing out the same course of events, reading the same lines in the same melodramatic, theatrical fashion, stuck in a "house of fiction". This house, with its patriarchal atmosphere and inescapable walls can be read as the symbol of a male dominated ideology from which the two women of the house cannot extricate themselves. Céline and Julie however are free of this constraint as they manage to disrupt the narrative flow of events in the play and even escape from the "house of fiction". Therefore, they escape patriarchal dominance.

If *Céline et Julie* is characterised by a direct, explicit interaction with narrative forms and structures, *Paris nous appartient* can be seen as a film which functions with only the illusion of a narrative structure. It is a feat in conjuring a drama out of nothing, a film which requires the illusion of plot in order to be held together but with no further use for it than that. In short, the film abides by the philosophy that "[t]o talk about a narrative is to create the effect of a narrative". The protagonist, Anna, becomes involved with a group of bohemians who may or may not be part of a secret underground political organisation. Her investigations into various happenings (the death of one of the members and the loss of a music tape of improvised guitar music) form the basis of what we see. Despite that, Anna seems to be completely guileless in her search as she is "propelled by means of deflected agendas, chance encounters, overheard and ill-understood phrases and fragments" which seem to lead her only to dead-ends. They provide no solutions and only raise more questions about the veracity of these happenings.

In discussing the film some fifteen years after its completion, Rivette lamented the fact that those who had seen it upon release had tried to approach it as a traditional narrative work; trying to decipher meaning from its cut-up narrative rather than observing the formal aspects of the narrative construction itself. He noted that at the end of the film, we know only one thing: that "[n]othing took place but the place". This reveals perhaps the most important effect that this inscrutable narrative structure achieves and that is of establishing the place itself, the city of Paris, as a major "character" in the film.

The importance of the role of the city is hinted at in the title. In English it is, "Paris belongs to us" and we assume at the beginning of the film that the "us" in the title refers to the group of bohemians whose activities we follow. The film, paradoxically, begins with an inter-title featuring a quote from French author Charles Peguy, "Paris belongs to no one". As the film develops, we begin to see that the Peguy quote is perhaps closer to the truth than the title of the film. The characters drift aimlessly from place to place in the city without any sort of narrative drive. They are lost in the space that envelops them. The Paris in which the young group lives appears to be constantly shifting from beneath their feet as there are almost as many different locations as there are scenes in the film. This uncanny, unhomely feel of the city is exemplified in a scene where Anna is crossing the road just beneath the Arc de Triomphe. The camera cuts back and forth between the Arc itself and her worried expression looking up at the structure. It is transformed from a symbol of triumph to some sort of surveillance monolith that Anne tries to shrink away from. One gets the feeling that all the talk of conspiracy and subterfuge is simply a reflection of the city's oppressive nature that affects the people who reside in it.

While the feeling of being "lost in space" creates an uneasy tension within the bohemian group, one could argue that the spectre of narrative looming over the group amplifies and exacerbates this tension into the realm of paranoia. Here, the "ghost" of a narrative manifests itself as a possible causal chain for the events that have happened. Have the mysterious disasters that have befallen the group been the doings of some sinister organisation or are they just pure coincidence? Film historian M.K. Raghavendra asserts that one who commits themselves to a narrative existence

… willingly assumes he [sic] is in the grip of processes outside of himself [sic], designed to do things to him [sic] that he [sic] will be powerless to resist. The instant that narrativity ceases is also the moment when life outside the narrative resumes …

This fear of living a narrative existence translates to a fear of the all-controlling "omniscient other", an apt metaphor for the Cold War paranoia which had gripped Western Europe so tightly during this period.

Ultimately, what makes these two films uniquely Rivettian is the challenge they pose to the viewer in attempting to reconcile avant-garde narrative forms with the creation of meaning. Both films invite us to explore the possibilities of non-traditional narrative structures in communicating different ideas and in doing so, they make us project our own thoughts and feelings into the cinematic worlds created by Jacques Rivette.

Works Cited

Johnson, W. 1974–1975. "Recent Rivette – An Inter-Re-View". *Film Quarterly*, Vol. 28, No. 2 (Winter): 32–39.

Kite, B. 2007. "Jacques Rivette and the Other Place, Track One". *Cinema Scope*, Vol. 30 (Spring): 12–21.

Lesage, J. 1981. "Celine and Julie Go Boating: Subversive Fantasy". *Jump Cut*, Vol. 24 (March): 10–25.

Marcorelles, L. 1958–59. "Paris nous appartient". *Sight and Sound*, Vol. 28., No. 1 (Winter): 4–6.

Milne, T. 1962. "Paris nous appartient". *Monthly Film Bulletin*, No. 343 (August): 33–36.

Neupert, R.A. 2007. *History of French New Wave Cinema*. Wisconsin: University of Wisconsin Press.

Raghavendra, M.K. 2007. "The World as Narrative: Interpreting Jacques Rivette". *Phalanx: A Quarterly Review for Continuing Debate*, No. 2: 13–26.

Rosenbaum, J. 1974. "Work and Play in the House of Fiction: On Jacques Rivette". *Sight and Sound*, Vol. 43 (Autumn): 190–94.

Rosenbaum, J., Sedofsky, L. & Adair, G. 1974. "Phantom Interviewers Over Rivette". *Film Comment*, Vol. 10, No. 6 (Sep/Oct): 18–24.

Watts, P. 2005. "Jacques Rivette's Classical Illusion". *Contemporary French and Francophone Studies*, Vol. 9, No. 3: 291–99.

Wood, R. 1981. "Narrative Pleasure: Two Films of Jacques Rivette". *Film Quarterly*, Vol. 35, No. 1 (Autumns): 2–12.

Filmography

Céline et Julie vont en bateau: Phantom Ladies Over Paris [Céline and Julie Go Boating] (1974). Jacques Rivette (192 minutes).

Paris nous appartient [Paris Belongs to Us] (1960). Jacques Rivette (140 minutes).

EPIC RIVALRY

Competition between Homer, Virgil and Lucan

Stephanie Morse

Homer is the undisputed king of ancient epic poetry and is thought of as the founder of all Western literature. His Roman successors, therefore, had enormous shoes to fill. The best writers use Homeric models to enhance their own works, placing themselves in direct competition with the progenitor. Virgil in his *Aeneid* and Lucan in his *Bellum Civile* are such poets that adopt and adapt Homeric prototypes. Lucan also had to respond to Virgil's immense influence on Roman epic. Through Virgil's imitation of the shield of Achilles, Lucan's parody of a hero's *aristeia* and the variations on the traditional epic contact with the underworld, it is evident that the literary descendants of the greatest classical writers both revered and challenged their legacy.

The shield of Aeneas in the *Aeneid* Book 8 closely engages with Homer's description of the shield of Achilles in Book 18 of the *Iliad*. The basic parallels are evident. Both shields are gifts from their divine mothers and forged by Hephaistos/Vulcan. They both have a similar structure of six scenes and a conclusion that has a reference to dancing, a ring of ocean and descriptions of the city at peace and at war (Penwill 2005, 38). Aeneas and Achilles are aligned with each other, emphasising Aeneas' role as the Achilles figure and undermining Turnus' claim to that title (Anderson 1957, 26). Although their origins and structures have close parallels, the details differ enormously. Achilles' shield is a microcosm of the Greek universe while Aeneas' shield is a representation of Roman history. Homer describes the shield as it is being made, using the present tense (Putnam 1998, 168) to depict scenes of daily life contemporary to Achilles and therefore completely comprehensible to him. Contrastingly, Virgil describes his shield as it is given to Aeneas, using primarily past tense (Putnam 1998, 168) to describe future events, connecting the past, present and future through this prophetic item (Kurman 1974, 6) and the hero is described as *"ignarus"*, ignorant or unaware. Achilles simply requires revenge on Hector. Aeneas unquestioningly shoulders the burden of his entire people and their future progeny (Clausen 1964, 142). Therefore, Virgil's account of the shield is placed in direct competition with his model.

However, these ekphrases serve entirely different purposes. Homer uses his shield as a relief from the intense and gory battle scenes surrounding it. This shows a wider world of human experience outside the realm of warfare (Homer 1987, xliv). In the *Aeneid*, however, the shield serves a wider ideological purpose. For positivist readings, it reinforces the pro-Augustan message pervading the poem (cf. Virgil 2003, xxix). However, the message from this most subtle and complex of Latin poets is surely more than simply laudatory. None of the scenes on the shield are explicitly commented on, leaving Aeneas and the audience to judge for themselves (Ross 2007, 114). Many of the scenes are in themselves problematic. For example, the rape of the Sabines and the cruel, savage punishment of Mettus are very morally questionable actions and are described as such in Livy's first book. Furthermore, a shadow could be cast over the pro-Augustan ideology during the Actium scene. Venus also seduces Vulcan into making the shield, which is quite different from Thetis calling in a favour. So while on the surface, the shield appears as purely glowing praise of Augustus. Virgil subtly implies that he like Vulcan was seduced into writing this description (Penwill 2005, 45). While we look to Augustan Rome as a Golden Age, Virgil is expressing doubts. For him the Golden Age is a hope or ideal, not necessarily yet a reality (Ross 2007, 117). The shield of Aeneas, therefore, plays an entirely different role in the *Aeneid* to the shield of Achilles in the *Iliad*. Virgil's shield, while not anti-Augustan, questions the values of Rome and its new ruler and simultaneously provides an optimistic view of the future. It slots in perfectly to the complex ideology and morals of the *Aeneid*.

Lucan's view of a depraved, morally bankrupt society turning its sword upon itself is completely at odds with Homer's heroic view of the world. Nowhere is this clearer than in the single Homeric *aristeia* in the *Bellum Civile*, that of Cassius Scaeva. In the *Iliad*, the driving force behind a warrior's decision to fight is a need for glory and everlasting fame (Clarke 2004, 77–78). Heroic combat is one-on-one and aristocratic (Rutherford 1996, 37), and there is a hierarchy of heroes on each side. Slain warriors die immediately, with only a select few permitted speech before death (Rutherford 1996, 39). The greatest omen is to fight for your country (Hom. *Il.* 12.243). This heroic and noble view of warfare is parodied in Scaeva's *aristeia*. He is '*bellum atque virum*' (Luc. 6. 191–92), one man against an army (Bramble 1982, 543). He is a soldier not an aristocrat (Ahl 1976, 117). Instead of dying immediately as was traditional and appropriate, he continues to fight long after he is struck, even surviving a blinding, before he is finally overwhelmed. Most importantly, Scaeva's military bravery, seemingly so like to the divinely inspired *aristeiai* of men like Achilles and Diomedes, is condemned in two lines: "eager for every wrong, he did not know how great a crime is valour in civil war" (Hardie 1993, 106–07). Lucan's directness here is completely in contrast with Homer and Virgil who allow the audience to make their own interpretations (Gorman 2001, 264–65).

This *aristeia* is also slightly different to any of Homer's. According to Homeric and Virgilian institutions of glory, a hero's glory is cumulative. When a greater hero in turn kills a hero, the sum total of the slain hero's glory is transferred to the conqueror (Gorman 2001, 265). Consequently, naming the victims is an essential part of traditional epic glory, as it allows for greater glory to be claimed by the victor. Thus, the fact that only one opponent of Scaeva is named is significant. Scaeva defeats his final opponent, Aulus, through treachery, not bravery, and the potential glory is hence nullified (Gorman 2001, 278-79). Lucan takes a Homeric tradition and reverses it, placing his own conception of the *aristeia* in competition with Homer's. Yet, Lucan's depiction of an *aristeia* is relevant to civil wars only and is thus an adaptation of rather than a challenge to Homeric ideals.

Necromancy (*nekyia*) or journeys to the underworld (*katabasis*) are conventional parts of ancient epic. Virgil and Lucan have significantly altered the archetypal contact with the underworld, epitomised in Book 11 of the *Odyssey*, in order to explore the major themes in their poems. Virgil Romanises the *nekyia* of Odysseus. Lucan undermines Virgil's depiction of the underworld to make one more suited to the turbulent and gruesome nature of the civil war.

Odysseus originally engaged in necromancy to bring the soul of Teiresias to the surface, so that he might prophesise the nature of Odysseus' return home. This he does (Hom. *Od.* 11.100-37); yet in the process, Odysseus opens a portal to the underworld. As a consequence, he sees the souls of a recently deceased companion, his mother, great women of Greek myth, his fellow warriors and the realms of Hades. The entire episode has an air of pathos and despair – the greatest of the dead, says Achilles, is worse than the lowliest life (Hom. *Od.* 489-91).

Aeneas parallels this structure in his journey into the underworld. He meets Palinurus who is substituting for Elpenor. The brooding Dido parallels Odysseus' sour encounter with Ajax. Aeneas talks to Deiphobus who tells a tale not unlike that of Agamemnon (Solmsen 1972, 35). The Sibyl takes the place of Circe, Anchises of Anticleia and Teiresias (Prescott 1963, 185). There are many similarities then. Yet, the differences are more illuminative of Virgil's purpose. The meeting with the dead prophet is delayed until the end because Aeneas is making a physical journey through the underworld, creating suspense and drama (Prescott 1963, 184). The catalogue of future Romans replaces the catalogue of mythic women. Rather than Achilles' bleak message about life after death, Anchises describes the model of rebirth, adapted from Stoic, Orphic and Platonic philosophy (Fletcher 1951, xii-xxviii). Thus, Aeneas' journey is much more positive and optimistic: he passes through the realms of the dead, reflecting on his own past, to the fields of Elysium which look towards the future (Williams 1964, 52). Aeneas also moves out of the Homeric heroic world and into the Roman system of values (Williams 1964, 63). Yet, as always with Virgil, there is a troubling undercurrent. The last person mentioned in the list of Romans is Marcellus, the recently deceased heir of Augustus. Then Aeneas leaves the underworld through the ivory gate of false dreams. The eulogy to Marcellus undercuts the triumphant tone of the Roman parade; the choices of participants, such as the Gracchi and the Drusi, reflect Virgil's wish for the audience to question the procession (Ahl 1976, 140-43). The ivory gate is also problematic. No satisfactory explanation has been found for this (Fletcher 1951, 101-02). So Virgil's vision of the underworld serves as a transition from the Odyssean half of the *Aeneid* to the Iliadic and from the Homeric Aeneas to the Roman. However, despite being much more positive that Homer's, it still presents complex and problematic themes.

Where Virgil's view is essentially an optimistic version of the afterlife, Lucan's is quite the opposite. The most monstrous and graphic depiction of necromancy in the ancient world is recorded in Book 6 of the *Bellum Civile*, that of Erichtho and Sextus Pompey, a fictional, supernatural event in an historical epic. This paradox can be seen as Lucan conforms to epic tradition while enhancing the horror of the imminent battle at Pharsalia, using the more realistic method of black magic as opposed to a corporeal appearance by the underworld (Martindale 1980, 370). While Aeneas and Odysseus approach the prophecies of the dead because they have been told they must, Sextus is merely afraid for himself and wishes to know his own future. This cowardice and his own evil corruption result in the horrifying described rites of necromancy and the resurrection of a corpse. Lucan translates Aeneas' burial of Misenus and his search for the golden bough into Erichtho's search for an unburied corpse. The rites of resurrection involve pouring blood back into a body as opposed to the letting of sacrificial blood (Masters 1992, 190–92). The corpse describes turmoil in the underworld. Here, Virgil's united catalogue of Romans is separated into inhabitants of Elysium and Tartarus. The segregation is done along purely political lines, with despairing republican people in Elysium and jubilant disturbers of the peace in Tartarus (Ahl 1976, 138). Sulla in Lucan's Elysium serves much the same purpose as the Gracchi and Drusi in Virgil's Roman parade. It satirises and complicates his picture of the underworld, causing the audience an uncomfortable moment of reflection (Ahl 1976, 139). The corpse prophesies about the destruction of the Pompeian line, where Anchises predicted the rise of the Roman line (Bartsch 2005, 500). The opposition of Lucan's *nekyia* to Virgil's *katabasis* is representative of the opposition of their poems as a whole. Virgil records the rise of Rome in an optimistic way, in contrast, Lucan emphasises the destruction of free Rome.

The competition between these three literary titans is apparent to any informed reader. The latter authors parallel and oppose their predecessors. Despite this competition, a judgement of value cannot truly be made between them, as the purposes of these imitations are not the same as their models. Virgil often parallels Homeric models but adapts them to his own complex morals by both questioning and affirming the Augustan age. Lucan presents a nihilistic, pessimistic view of the civil war, lampooning Homeric and Virgilian values to undercut their more optimistic views of the world. In doing so he becomes an anti-Virgil (Conte 1994, 443). In spite of the similarities of these scenes, they cannot be measured against one another. Instead they should be appreciated in their own contexts. All four poems are valuable works of literature and they complement and challenge one another without entering into direct competition.

Primary Sources

Lucan. 1992. *Civil War*. Translated by Braund, S.H. Oxford: Oxford University Press.

Livy. 2002. *The Early History of Rome*. Translated by De Sélincourt, A. London: Penguin Books.

Homer. 1987. *The Iliad*. Translated by Hammond, M. London: Penguin Books.

Homer. 1980. *The Odyssey*. Translated by Shewring, W. Oxford: Oxford University Press.

Virgil. 2003. *The Aeneid*. Translated by West, D. London: Penguin Books.

Works Cited

Ahl, F.M. 1976. *Lucan: An Introduction*. Ithaca: Cornell University Press.

Anderson, W.S. 1957. "Virgil's Second *Iliad*." *Transactions and Proceedings of the American Philological Association*, 88: 17–30.

Bartsch, S. 2005. "Lucan." In *A Companion to Ancient Epic*. Edited by J.M. Foley. Malden: Blackwell Publishing.

Bramble, J.C. 1982. "Lucan." In *The Cambridge History of Classical Literature II: Latin Literature*. Edited by E.J. Kenney and W.V. Clausen, 533–57.

Clarke, M. 2004. "Manhood and Heroism." In *The Cambridge Companion to Homer*. Edited by R. Fowler, 74–90.

Clausen, W. 1964. "A Interpretation of the Aeneid." *Harvard Studies in Classical Philosophy*, 68: 139-47.

Conte, G.B. 1994. *Latin Literature: A History*. Translated by J.B. Solodow. Baltimore: The John Hopkins University Press.

Fletcher, F. 1951. *Virgil: Aeneid VI*. Oxford: Clarendon Press.

Gorman, V.B. 2001. "Lucan's Epic *Aristeia* and the Hero of the *Bellum Civile*." *CJ*, 96.3: 263-90.

Hardie, P. 1993. *The Epic Successors of Virgil: A Study in the Dynamics of a Tradition*. Cambridge: Cambridge University Press.

Kurman, G. 1974. "Ecphrasis in Epic Poetry." *Comparative Literature*, 26.1: 1-13.

Martindale, C.A. 1980. "Lucan's Nekuia." In *Studies in Latin Literature & Roman History II*. Edited by C. Deroux, 367-77. Brussels: Latomus.

Masters, J. 1992. *Poetry and Civil War in Lucan's* Bellum Civile. Cambridge: Cambridge University Press.

Penwill, J.L. 2005. "Reading Aeneas' Shield." *Iris: Journal of the Classical Association of Victoria*, 18: 37-47.

Prescott, H.W. 1963. *The Development of Virgil's Art*. New York: Russell & Russell Inc.

Putnam, M.C.J. 1998. *Virgil's Epic Designs: Ekphrasis in the* Aeneid. New Haven: Yale University Press.

Ross, D.O. 2007. *Virgil's* Aeneid: *A Reader's Guide*. Malden: Blackwell Publishing.

Rutherford, R.B. 1996. *Homer*. Greece & Rome: New Surveys in the Classics 26. Oxford: Oxford University Press.

Solmsen, F. 1972. "The World of the Dead in Book 6 of the *Aeneid*." *Classical Philosophy*, 67: 31–41.

Williams, R.D. 1964. "The Sixth Book of the *Aeneid*." *Greece and Rome (Second Series)*, 11.1: 48–63.

NOTE TO SHAKESPEARE

Symonne Torpy

———

You couldn't feel my breathing,

I could not feel my own.

I'd taken precious poison

So I'd never be alone.

The deal had been an open crypt,

But Romeo missed the note.

I'm fluttering my eyelids,

But it seems I've missed the boat.

I've entered into storage,

There's no recovery card,

So as I'm being buried

I'm writing out the Bard.

———

In silent protest I lay still,

My mind's cogs turning 'round,

Hotspur and Polonious

You wrote into the ground!

And what about poor Regan,

Hamlet or Mercutio?

Did you seek permission

Before forcing them to go?

Shakespeare, go and fuck thine self,

Or ending it would do.

I'm sending J.K. Rowling,

As playwright in your lieu.

So what? Her ending's soppy,

A corporate writing deal;

But did you pause to wonder,

How Juliet would feel?

TWO BIRDS (DANCING) ON A WIRE

Audrey Menezes

And then I'm jumping
Jumping
While wearing your jumper
And I'm laughing and thinking of your blueberry shorts
Patriotic for me, your only country
Starred with the red of my lips
And I'm thinking of the time when we mixed up our names
And how, now, we smile untangled at each other from across the room
Our looks skipping across bent elbows scattered through
(Skip back and then look away because we are not friends, you & I)

But I like to jumpjumpjump in just this way
And I like to hop
Lithely from hipbone to hipbone
For I am searching for a bed that is as warm as your jumper
And shorts that are as intimately warm
And a ribcage that fits and locks tightly into the spaces of my own
I will happily balance when I am all mixed up

CANIDAE

Laura Senkewitz

———

We live under the old stone bridge

Where the passenger trains go over every day,

Carrying lives to their destinations. Late Sunday night

The goods train rumbles over, its trucks filled with crates

Of cans and bottles, and rattles to a stop.

As the driver takes a break, takes a beer

From the crate in the nearest truck, takes a leak

In the bushes behind the stationmaster's hut.

We prowl up the hill, brushing through the long grass.

The last four trucks have come

From the Sunday markets, and are fat with rubbish.

We scratch through the wrappers and papers for food scraps.

In the last truck there is a man, sluggish

With alcohol and poverty, dozing amongst the garbage.

He wakes to see us closing in; the moonlight glints

Off his fear-filled eyes. He begins to move,

But too late. We are swift and hungry

For fresh meat, and drag him down the hill,

Under the bridge. Nobody will notice

He is gone.

The sun has risen high over the hill, and flies buzz

And scamper in the warm puddles of thickening blood.

We sleep in the shadow of the stones,

And wait for our next meal.

LIOR

Arghya Gupta

———

I'm a cigar trade con. On Golden eve, stuck

O ... Dial tone ... tile rot!

Cod liver oil prawn I am

Mega Female Illicit Sale Time!!!

Seen keg are vases

Om ... Amen

Ice ... rats – L.A. Cola?!

I yob mopedly;

"Who won't call an emo?"

"Whose–?" Oh! Spans I demand on women of Lahore

Zero ... half ... one.

Mow, *Nod* – Named, I snap shoes – oh women!

All act now

———

Oh Wylde –

Pom boy I, a local, stare – Cinema! "Moses"

Average knees emit elastic lie.

Lame fag.

Emma … In wrap; Lior, evil doctor, elite.

Not laid, ok!

Cuts evened log, No!

No cedar tragic am I.

UNKNOWN I

Raihana Haidary

———

In the winds of yesterday, beneath the horizon of tomorrow, I stand once more.

I feel the crisp air, the faint breeze, a breath of life in this lifeless world. The fine green soil scatters its wretched soul, a speckled world. Red ... painted across the sky. Isolation oozes from Thear – Earth's deformed foetus. I long for the mother's yellow warmth, the blue blanket that once wrapped her visitors. A hollow sound travels through Thear's soul. I turn around ... nothing. Nothing but the red and the green, and the dust. Was there... is there ... any? And me? Questions ... the thirst for answers. Words roll off dry lips ... and the dust-caked ground takes me back. To moments, to worlds ... to civilisations. Alone. The last ...

... And the last shall be first ...

***

We seek to conquer the universe ... but we cannot control a small measure of land, or air, or space.

Red. A thick blood red erased the sky and the ground. Land and sea. I ran faster into the heart of the city, as the ground swirled beneath my feet. Pillar after pillar, materialising before being swallowed back into the red. I slowed down ... my breath uneven. Dust scratched the back of my throat, staining my vision, settling upon my cracked lips. Silence except the arrhythmic

———

heartbeat. I felt invisible. I turned up, searching for her grace. But the blue had become red. The sky became the ground.

As the red choked the air, swallowed the sea, I was aware of only me. But the birds stood still, firmly, on their branches. The trees had become the final defence, not a branch bowed in defeat as the wind mercilessly shook it to its core. Nature and Man. Are we but a product of our environment, or is our environment a product of us?

Climate change … change … renewal … renewable…each false hope blinded us to reality. She was withering away … how could we signal the death of our mother, Earth? The glass windows … smeared with red dust. Pieces of brick… of dried mud … crunched beneath the soles of my feet. The crimson red became orange … yellow … and blue once more.

***

These faint images fade as I sit down on Thear's ground. A piece of a jigsaw to slot together. A dust storm on a once blue haven. Moments pass but Thear's sky remains blood red, his soil still and as speckled green as before. So we had no choice? So we had to come? Of all places – here? The questions and the thirst for answers linger on my lips as I move through the red and green … searching… squinting for something, for someone. And a familiar nerve tingles within. Once …

***

In these chaotic times, why do I still stand alone? Why aren't our hands clasped when tragedy sweeps the land? So this is humanity?

Mother Earth's terminal illness echoed in the damp, cluttered streets. The icy water dripped off my body, the mud blurred my sight. Shaken, awaken.

Her soul silent, pale, as that almighty wave surged towards the heavens and drowned Earth. I felt the swallowed whole ... the barrier between nature and man removed as we became one. It painted the world brown and a deathly white. The trees ... pieces of debris ... bodies ... me. The people floundered, struggling to survive. A wretched scream ... a groan ... and then silence. No hands were raised for help, as if knowing none existed. I couldn't raise mine.

Create. If life cannot be savoured, it is not a life. You are not alive.

In a dimly lit room, I feel my fingers shaking uncontrollably, reaching for destiny. I took out the news clipping, his sheet of paper, warily, as if signing Earth's death certificate. I brought it across to the flickering light. The words remained etched across the sodden page. I breathed ...

Office of the World General
United Countries of the West

25th April 2020

I, A. S.

Believe that in the best interests of the entire human race – both Easterners and Westerners, immediate and effective action must be taken. My team and I have data from reliable sources that inform us of the perilous state of the planet that deteriorates day by day. As the world mourns the millions of victims in the terrible dust, water and fire catastrophes that have shaken the planet, we seek a permanent resolution.

I hereby give NASA permission to utilise his research skills and knowledge of the intergalactic planetary system to undertake whatever measures he sees fit to find a habitable state for as many people as possible.

If NASA is successful, I am to be informed of the conditions and the number of people that could possibly exist in such an environment.

If under any circumstances, NASA is unsuccessful in this mission, no such information is to be revealed to the public.

Sincerely,

A. S.
World General for the West

The words still lingered on my lips, my hollow voice echoed across the bunker. I folded the page three times before stuffing it into my left pocket. I swivelled over to my TEST table, scouring the hundreds of diagrams, thousands of research sheets. Book upon book of useless facts. Useless information. No such cure for PLANET ILLNESS existed. No such planet was ever built to facilitate the billions.

***

Breathe. Slowly, I place my hand within that very same pocket. I feel a small, thick piece of paper and take it out, carefully unfolding it. A brown, yellowish colour. The news-ink has run off the page, the "A.S." now a smudge. I turn the page over. Nothing ... but a few scribbles – almost illegible.

"Solar System inadequate.
Too hot, too cold. Create own planet? Too risky.
Womb-foetus, harness the biodiversity.
Thear -> a new Earth?"

Images flash before me as I desperately cling onto memories ... hopes ... dreams ... The birth of a deformed planet, the death of a loved one. Humanity's final endeavour. As discoverers, we searched for her jewels, her rare beauty. We then ravaged her body, dried the oil out of her soul to sweeten our lives, to fuel our thirst for more. Now she was used. Unwanted. She gave birth to the heroes who now became her enemy. I search deep within the images cluttering my mind, searching ... searching ...

***

"Mr Peter, you are well aware of your limitations! My office and I only seek an environment to replace Earth, not a race to replace humanity!"

His voice echoed. Just imagine – the pursuit of happiness would be replaced by pure joy! Isolation, suffering, pain ... all wiped away. Our dreams, finally within our grasp, never to escape, never to be cruelly snatched away. I hung onto the image. I felt my lip trembling, my tongue quivering. He would soon see.

"Of course, General." I lied. I rolled up the sheet, a nod, an ecstasy override.

***

We seek to challenge what we call a destiny, but we cannot even form our desired paths.

The last remnants of civilisation wither away on the false green soil, the dirt brown grass. The destination changes, but the traveller remains the same. The thirst for change has dried up ... into the fragments of dust that choke Thear's air. Pieces of the puzzle, faint images, form a picture. I open my cracked lips, a hollow sound emerges.

"Hello?"

The echo wafts through the air, lost in the winds of yesterday. I walk over to the horizon of tomorrow, jaded by the false, man-made plants that soar above into nothingness. A groan, a rumble emerges from Thear's soul. A soft wind carries the green soil, the crumpled letter ... carries me.

... And the last shall be first ...

CIGARETTE

Josie M

Worldliness personified, in one sphere.

The sphere in which you are an icon,

A symbol.

Where song after song on a single album gives you mention;

Where, as an accessory to a young urchin, with blisteringly red lipstick, you give a certain panache, a hint at the way we are to understand her.

Your allure; almost as strong as hers, and much stronger than her.

Light, warmth; lifting the experience to new heights, you live on, an irony of your effect, and in defiance of what the chain-smoker might think of you when the pack is out.

You are never gone.

Perhaps you yourself are an addict.

So easily twirled between the fingers – who is really in control?

So small and so potent; so powerful, so seemingly omnipresent.

In the other sphere you are just a man's habit.

A dirty pile in the streets; reduced to a heap of ash out on the balcony;

Perhaps even a taboo, hidden from those who do not embrace this form of worldliness as he does.

Clutching, or loosely balancing — it's all embracing.

In this sphere, you have only a shadowy resemblance of what you were in that world to which you are the key; only a hint of the way we understood you.

Perhaps, cigarette, were we not mutually killing each other,

I would be less dependent on you, and more fond.

FIRE

Tim Scriven

———

When Prometheus gave us our fire

He took our water

And to drink

We became vampires

Till the feast of cannibals

Ran dry

We burnt

On fields of flame

While the Gods,

Bitter-sweetly,

Oh-so-discretely

Laughed nervously

———

UNKNOWN II

Raihana Haidary

We were one ... but we were many.

I moved like clockwork.

Paper-Fold-Glue.

...

Paper-Fold-Glue.

I stole a lick from the salty moisture poised on my upper lip as beads of sweat slid like marbles down my arched back. I observed the girl opposite me, her tiny brown fingers submerged in the viscous glue. She took a sheet; her fingers trembling as she accurately outlined the matchbox. Then a few more boxes. She grabbed the razor that left its marks over her grubby hands and cut the shapes out. Her oiled plait swayed as she gathered her utensils. Glue. She scooped it with one finger and dragged it along the square. A thick layer of dirt was caked to her palms. I did not know her name. I did not know any of their names. Yet as we sat together on the stone floor, as our saris and loincloths touched each other – we were one.

He stepped closer to our circle and tapped his watch. Hurry. My fingers shook as I desperately tried to perfect my boxes.

I could not steal their lunch. I unlocked my numbed feet, the creaking bones turning heads. He lowered his wooden stick, bringing it towards my thighs before ... He drew back his stick, staring at the large bag of matchboxes under my arm. I walked over to the head officer's table. Inspection.

He clicked his tongue.

"Too slow."

He merely glanced at the bag, drew a box out and stopped.

"It is not straight. Will this sell? I can only feed you if you work for it. No rotis for anyone 'till 5."

I heard the sounds of tiny hands stop.

...

The buzzing resumed. It took time for the tears to trickle down my face. The girl opposite me reached for another sheet and felt a drop on her hand. She turned and placed her hand on mine and squeezed it softly. I smiled. We were a chain of dirty children. United ...

***

Routine. Every action became dictated by the looming hands of the clock. Every movement was calculated, every emotion mundane.

5:50pm

I was lost amongst the moving bodies. Like fragments of dust we humans seemed scattered about. I slithered through the hundreds navigating myself on this seemingly never-ending road. I kept my head up, and never looked down. I suffocated in this false sense of community. Each person blindly ran towards a destination that merely led on to yet another destination. And another. Nobody paused. The clock's hands moved again.

5:55pm

"Chalo, hurry! ..." they yelled.

I quickened my pace, ticket ready in hand.

6:00pm

The whistle grew faint in my ears. I became captured, not by the thirty odd fellow commuters cramped together like odd pieces of a puzzle in the train, but by the tiny fingers squeezing through the bars of the window. His grin pleaded at the passenger on board. Only a tiny rupee.

"No." The passenger looked away.

The boy's tiny feet ran until he couldn't keep up with the train. He loosened his grip on the bars. I turned away. Consumed by our own survival we forget that the hand we reach for only exists if we offer our hand to others. I looked down at my palms. It was the cursed hand that only extended itself for crumpled sheets of paper. I searched for the answers that lay in my questions. We cannot be one when the wind blows ...

***

Invisibility was power. Wrapped in a cream shawl and thin sari, sitting still with my eyes lowered I became transparent to the commuters. Hidden under my shawl, were the intricate silver and gold ornaments that encased my hands. They shook with the train. I hugged myself to prevent my anklets from chiming. To their eyes I was a mere speck on the canvas on which we were all painted.

Slowing down …

"Madam, what time is it?" one commuter bellowed to the lady opposite him.

"Seven"

Destiny called. I ran off the train – its wheels still in motion – the chime of my anklets turned heads. Past the crowded station that like a magnet, drew in hundreds. I ran through the streets – weaving around stalls, dodging pedestrians and vehicles. Faces became a blurred kaleidoscope.

"Maya!" screamed Aunty. "Maya it's almost time."

I stepped in through the back door. She wrinkled her nose at the sight of my sari in tatters.

"How about I give you nothing but a towel next time. Or will you ruin that too?" She grimaced.

I pulled the sari off and slipped into gold silk. Deftly I wove marigolds through my hair and tied ornaments that jangled, to my wrists. I dipped my feet into a shallow bowl of water, wiping away the fibres of the factory and the dust of the streets. I then carefully slid some rings onto my toes.

"Ready?"

I cast a final swift but piercing glance in the chipped mirror … red bindii – the final touch.

Behind the curtains, lying upon lustrous rugs an audience awaited. For me. With the hum of the sitar I began to twirl, pouring out the acrid contents of my heart. I was lost in the melody. Here.

UNKNOWN III

May Ling Ho

I was meant for a different time

I know that now

Ella sits opposite me

Her voice

So beautiful

Fills my head

"April In Paris ... "

"What have you done to my heart?"

I close my eyes

Piano blues wash over me

Every pore and nerve tingles – sensation

Ella's voice

Resonating

"I never knew my heart could sing"

Louis answers

Yes

Relaxed Free No Complications Heavenly

Sing that trumpet Louis

A trill and two long notes

Feel every note

Resonating

In the pit of my stomach

Tears

Is there such a place?

Where is it?

Ella returns to me

"April In Paris…"

"What have you done to my heart?"

I was not meant to be here

I know that now.

TIME TO AXE THE HSC ENGLISH SYLLABUS

Doug Brown

———

Controversy erupted during last year's HSC English exam when one of the questions was modified from its traditional format. Students were asked to write about one additional text instead of the usual two. This seemingly minor change was positively revolutionary and debilitating for the thousands of students who had prepared their responses to the examination questions based on the precedents established over the last decade of HSC English papers. Anecdotal evidence suggested that many confused students simply proceeded to reproduce their prepared essay with two additional texts, rather than apply their knowledge and modify their response even with the consequence of losing marks for incorrectly answering the question.

It seems this may have been a deliberate ploy from the Board of Studies (BOS) to "catch out" students who had rote-learned essays based on past trends in the exam questions. If so, it cruelly made an example out of this year's cohort in order to set standards for subsequent exams. The BOS showed no regard for the performance or stress levels of the teenage students sitting the most important exams of their lives. Additionally it shunned the

———

straightforward alternative of issuing a press release or advising teachers that the format of the exam would change. The President of the BOS, Tom Alegounarias, instead tried to shift the blame onto the students, arguing that they were responsible for turning the exams into a "memorising test". However, the BOS is the sole organisation responsible for turning HSC English into the farce that it is today.

There are two reasons why students prepare their responses for the HSC English exam. The first reason is that an ambitiously large number of texts are assessable for each part of the course, so the questions must be very broad and generic in order to cater for every possible permutation of studies. This of course limits the range of questions the examiners can ask and means that there is little variation in questions from year to year. Thus, it is advantageous for students to prepare responses, since the questions are so inherently predictable.

Secondly, the course has become far too challenging, and students are bewildered if they do not prepare responses. Consider, for example, the question on the Shakespearean play *King Lear*. Not only do students have to discuss traditional foci of study such as narrative, characterisation, themes, structure and language techniques, but they also have to analyse critical interpretations of the play. Students also needed to consider multiple productions of the play, and also – most frighteningly – "deconstruct" the play from the perspectives of multiple literary theories such as Marxism, feminism, post-structuralism, postmodernism, Freudianism, colonialism and anarchism. Most third-year university students would have difficulty with a question like this, let alone pimply teenagers in year twelve. It is no wonder that Melina Marchetta, author of the prescribed text *Looking for Alibrandi*, asserts "students today are required to do what most adults, including the Prime Minister, academics, parents, teachers and the writers of the actual texts, would find almost impossible to do, especially under HSC exam conditions."

Why has HSC English become so difficult? The answer is that the teaching of English has been influenced by the nefarious theory of postmodernism. Postmodernism is an abstract academic theory that contends that there is no such thing as objective truth or validity; reality is "socially constructed". In other words, there are no right or wrong answers since everything is "relative". Academic subjects are not distinct and therefore all courses must be interdisciplinary. Hence, traditional interpretations of *Lear* are "biased" and must be placed in context from the perspective of enlightened literary theories – all of which are relative – so that the red walls used in a famous production of *Lear* can symbolise either the proletarian ethos (Marxism) of the play or else signify the inherent passion of the female characters (feminism), according to your own subjective "reading" of the play (Or, maybe the colouring of the walls is irrelevant?). Thus, English classes no longer teach just books, poems and plays, but rather teach "texts" which encompass "sound, print, film, electronic and multimedia representations", meaning that cultural studies, visual arts, music, film studies, performance studies and marketing are now essential components of English. Furthermore, SMS messages, twitters, websites and advertisements are considered to have the same literary "value" as the traditional literature. In past HSC questions, students have been asked to analyse photographs, posters, CD-Rom covers, PowerPoint presentations, websites, visual texts and visual arts reviews. Traditionalists may well ponder why literary theories developed hundreds of years after the death of Shakespeare – and basing their interpretation on spurious evidence such as the colouring of walls – have any currency with the authors of the syllabus. They may also ask why the grand English canon is being superseded by today's degenerate iPhone/Facebook culture.

The most notorious feature of postmodernist writing is the reliance on verbose, incomprehensible language in an effort to disguise the complete irrationality of the theory. The HSC English syllabus, a document which is designed to clarify the expected outcomes and requirements for students does just that. If you wished to know the definition of "meaning", it is provided:

> **Meaning:** The dynamic relationship between text and responder involving information (explicit and implicit), the affective and the contextual

If that is not clear enough, the syllabus elaborates by defining meaning "in and through texts":

> **Meaning in and through texts:** This expression implies that meaning variously
> · resides in texts
> · is a dynamic process through which responders engage with texts, and
> · involves the incorporation of understanding gained through texts into a wider context.

If you wished to know the definition of "textual integrity" – a word entirely invented by the syllabus to form an "artificial language" according to former Board of Studies President Gordon Stanley – you need only look up the glossary of the syllabus:

> **Textual integrity:** the unity of a text; its coherent use of form and language to produce an integrated whole in terms of meaning and value.

You will be thankful you did look up that term, because it has featured in past exam questions.

I sat the HSC exams in 2006 and recall my own problems with the loquacious language of the syllabus. In one assessment, I was asked to discuss "how language forms, features and the structures of texts shape meaning and influence response". When I queried my teacher as to the meaning of that ridiculous request, I was told simply "it means language techniques". When I asked him why he couldn't have just said this in the wording of the question, he replied that he had to "jump through hoops" to satisfy the outcomes of the syllabus.

Not only do students have no idea what is expected of them in the course, they are also being unduly influenced by the postmodernist language style of the syllabus, in the belief that it is necessary to maximise marks. To quote Adam, an HSC graduate in 2005, English has become a "competition to see who can out-bullshit each other" with ever-more ridiculous postmodernist jargon and language distortions. English teacher James King advises students to:

> throw in a few names like Jacques Derrida or Roland Barthes (famous postmodernists) and use the words "discourse" and "intertextuality" as often as possible. You need not know what any of it means ...

A student blogger confirmed this popular exam strategy:

> We received lists of acceptable "buzzwords" to use, stock sentences for the beginning and end of paragraphs, and were told almost uniformly that we would get "points" every time a marker saw the word juxtapositioning ...

Unfortunately, this style of teaching has not fostered the necessary writing skills in HSC English graduates, as Sydney University academic Dr Barry Spurr laments:

> among the bright students who go on to university, their ability to express themselves orally and in writing is woeful. They have

not been trained properly in language and they haven't had to stretch themselves in terms of expressing themselves clearly and intelligently. It's enough to "respond" to these texts ...

The focus on literary theories has so substantially eroded traditional education in English that students need not even read the texts anymore. As English teacher James King notes, published answers that received marks in the top 5% of the state made not a single reference to a character or event in a comparative question on the novel *Brave New World* and the film *Blade Runner*. Regarding my own studies, I barely read any of the books set for study, and knew next to nothing about the plotlines or characters featured in the novels. Yet, I managed to score in the top bands in both my English courses by relying on *Excel* study guides and the website boredofstudies. org, where students upload their work in a file-sharing community. Anecdotal evidence also suggests many students pay their tutors to write their essays, which they either submit for written assessments or rote-learn in preparation for the exam.

A responder to this essay might argue that students should just accept that the course is difficult and not enrol in it if they can not handle it. However, English is the only course in the HSC that is mandatory, and even the weaker students who enrol in English Standard must still deal with this postmodernist nonsense in one of the four modules of the course – the two-hour Area of Study exam, which raised so much controversy this year. Furthermore, it is literally impossible for students of English Standard to score a mark in the top band (90 and above) because of the practice of scaling, and so a student who endeavours to do well academically must either enrol in the excessively difficult English Advanced course, or else accept their fate and cringe when the UAC letter arrives.

It is now time to scrap the HSC English syllabus, and replace it with a plain English document that expresses clearly what outcomes are expected of students. At base, the course should focus on teaching the most important and useful English skills of reading and writing, in adequate preparation for further studies. Traditional, canonical texts should be the essence of the course, and complex critical theory and literary criticism should be abandoned because of their difficulty, with an emphasis on the staples of narrative, characterisation, themes, structures and language techniques. Teachers and examiners should scrutinise the writing of students, with the teaching of plain English skills such as style, spelling, grammar and punctuation which are the cornerstones of the course. To conclude, I believe the exams should be modified to more closely resemble the Year 10 School Certificate English exam, with more questions addressing unseen texts to ensure students' analytical skills are genuine and not prefabricated or plagiarised.

Bibliography

Board of Studies NSW 2009. *English Syllabus*, 2 October, [Online], Available: www.boardofstudies.nsw.edu.au/syllabus_hsc/pdf_doc/english-syllabus-from2010.pdf [28 July 2010].

Bye, C. 2003. "How the Internet Earns Top Mark". *Sydney Morning Herald*, 21 December, [Online], Available: http://www.smh.com.au/articles/2003/12/20/1071868698254.html [28 July 2010].

Horin, A. 2009. "English by Numbers – Students Find Formula for HSC Success". *Sydney Morning Herald*, 31 October, [Online], Available: www.smh.com.au/opinion/society-and-culture/english-by-numbers--students-find-formula-for-hsc-success-20091030-hppm.html [28 July 2010].

King, J. 2002. "This Is Not a Headline, It's An HSC English Exam Text". *Sydney Morning Herald*, 3 September, [Online], Available: www.smh.com.au/articles/2002/09/02/1030953435609.html [28 July 2010].

Marchetta, M. 2006. "HSC English is Tough and Smarter, Not Dumb and Dumber". *Sydney Morning Herald*, 1 May, [Online], Available: www.smh. com.au/news/opinion/hsc-english-is-tough-and-smarter-not-dumb-and-dumber/2006/04/30/1146335609488.html [28 July 2010].

Norrie, J. 2005. "Alas, Poor Students … ". *Sydney Morning Herald*, 15 August, [Online], Available: www.smh.com.au/news/national/alas-poor-studen ts-8230/2005/08/14/1123957949797.html [28 July 2010].

Orwell, G. 1946. "Politics and the English Language". *Horizon*, April, [Online], Available: orwell.ru/library/essays/politics/english/e_polit [28 July 2010].

Patty, A. 2009. "Tables Turned on HSC Students", *Sydney Morning Herald*, 2 November, [Online], Available: www.smh.com.au/national/tables-turned-on-hsc-students-20091101-hrlg.html [28 July 2010].

SEXUALITY IS VIOLENCE

Coital Coercion and Romeo and Juliet

Patrick O'Sullivan

————

Two households, like at least in simile,
In fair Verona where the scene is set:
Wet with Violence and Sexuality:
Grudge forbids love, so love grows in secret,
An' a pair of star-cross'd lovers take their life:
A silly act of unbridled passion,
But unalterable end to constant strife?
Forewarned from the start, after a fashion.
But Lust and Ire look to be examined
Within the traffic of the next few leaves,
As it interacts, and acts on these condemned
(Where innuendo comes as thick as thieves).
For never did a story bode more threat
Than this of Romeo and his Juliet

If love be rough with you, be rough with love;
Prick love for pricking and you beat love down.

From the prologue of Shakespeare's classic, *Romeo and Juliet*, the close relationship that is played out between violence and sexuality can be seen. It is told that "A pair of star-cross'd lovers take their life", and hence the tension between these two themes is introduced. The interplay between sexuality and violence, where sexuality pervades violent situations and where violence is infused into the sexual scenes occurs both in a considered and subtle manner and on an obvious vulgar level, particularly among men. At the same time witty banter may cloud the sexuality and/or violence in a jocular aspect especially from Mercutio and heartfelt exchanges distract from the underlying fear of exploitation and even outright rape. So violent attitudes toward sexuality are examined within the social context of the play, as well as in a literary comparison.

The initial scene, Act I, Sc I, sets up a paradigm for the rest of the play with the introduction of the masculine culture. The scene is set with Gregory and Sampson, two men of the house of Capulet, talking about manly things. They discuss maintaining honour in society, honour in battle and end talking on sexual conduct (lines 1–30). This short exchange foregrounds a number of aspects pertinent to the action of the play, namely pervasive violence stemming from the "ancient grudge" between the Montagues and Capulets and the sexuality that is constantly upon the mind of all in the play. The nature of the banter prepares the audience for the constant competition in conversation, particularly in other homosocial situations, where each character tries to outwit the other. This occurs even between these two friends. Each line exchanged in the dialogue feeds from the previous where a pun is drawn. Each character tries to demean and dominate the other. The conversation begins simply that an offence to honour will not be tolerated from anyone ("we'll not carry coals" l. 1). This quickly shifts to bravery and skill when fighting. "A dog of that house", (l. 10) introduces the image of dumb obedience to a master though clearly applies to retainers of either household.

Furthermore, it serves to illustrate the bestial nature of violence and enmity between the two houses. The dialogue turns to Sampson who is trying to convey his macho masculinity amid Gregory's questioning his rebuttals.

While the themes of conversation are hardly foreign to a contemporary audience, it becomes a bit controversial even in modern times when the conversation shifts to sexually preying upon women:

> Samp. ... *therefore I will push Montague's men from the wall, and thrust his maids to the wall.*

> Greg. *The quarrel is between our masters and us their men.*

What Gregory is conveying here is the separation of women from the violence and there is dishonour in the action of raping the Montague women. In Sampson's innuendoes masochism is displayed, which may be perpetrated by the "gentlemen" of these houses.

In Gregory's later continuation of the idea of sexually assaulting the women ("They must take it in sense that feel it" l. 26) – after initially challenging it – this dishonourable violence is extended to be possible from any and all. This reinforces the Machiavellian stereotype of the Italian that was prevalent in Elizabethan England. While charming, Italians cannot be trusted and will use any means to achieve their ends, also illustrated by Shakespeare as Jachimo in *Cymbeline*. Thus, the concept that this perfect and wholesome romantic ideal, superficially observable in the love between Romeo and Juliet, may be tainted and liberally laced with an underlying violence. This display of masculinity is also shown in Romeo's fight with Tybalt. The phallic and sexual imagery in the sword fight might be transferable to Romeo's relationship with Juliet. Initially because of his love for Juliet his manhood has been compromised ("Thy beauty hath made me effeminate / And in my temper softened valour's steel" III.I l. 116-17). Consequentially, he overly asserts his masculinity by stabbing Tybalt with his rapier before fulfilling the metaphor with Juliet.

In Act II, Scene II the audience experiences a level of voyeurism that is often overlooked or ignored when the scene is studied, but if Actaeon was guilty then certes Romeo is. Part of this may be the reputation of the scene as the epitome of romance, a preconceived idea which the audience must remove itself from. The scene begins with the young lover breaking into his love's/ desire's house and peering at her in secret. It has been reconstructed in the television show *Skins* when Tony, attempting to makeup with his (ex-) girlfriend quotes lines 3–5 and lines 10–13,

> It is the east and Juliet is the sun! / Arise fair sun and kill the envious moon / Who is already sick and pale with grief … It is my lady, O it is my love! / O that she knew she were! / She speaks, yet she says nothing. What of that? / Her eye discourses. I will answer it.

This illustrates the superficial understanding of the scene as eloquent poetry expressing innocent and virtuous love. Yet, what audiences should realise is that, just like Tony in the serial, Romeo might just be manipulative, wanting Michelle/Juliet as a conquest rather than true love. This is a real threat for Juliet made even more dangerous by Romeo eavesdropping in on her monologue where she expresses her love for him. He knows exactly the influence he wields over her emotionally. The problem comes for audiences when Romeo is seemingly excused for his voyeuristic behaviour because of the risk involved. Later Juliet admits her love for him and then they finally have a romantic exchange when Romeo reveals himself. It is a wonder that these act as defences when, considered, they all sensibly condemn the lusty lover. Capulet surely would not like enemy Montagues sneaking into his house, especially where they may rape his daughter, even more so if the daughter is seduced willingly to humiliate and shame the family honour. In Act II, Scene II, Romeo might be seen to pursue a different method of courtship, unlike the conventional – that which with Rosaline ended in his rejection. Parallels between the two objects of Romeo's desire can be drawn: When Romeo describes to Benvolio his dismissal by Rosaline he says, "She will not stay the siege of loving terms", (Act I, Scene I, l. 210).

This is then remedied with Juliet in the physical act of overcoming her household walls. Romeo creates (accidentally) a distinct (and morbid) connection when he refers to death piloting his life in Act I, Scene IV, l. 112, "But he [death] hath the steerage of my course / Direct my suit". In answer to Juliet's questioning how he came to be at her window Romeo says, "I am no pilot, yet wert thou as far / As that vast shore wash'd with the farthest sea, / I should adventure for such merchandise" (l. 82–84). In the footnote to Act I, Scene IV, l. 113, attention is drawn to different rendering of the word here printed "suit", which may be exchanged for "saile" in some editions. In contrast, Dr Samuel Johnson's note to this is that suit refers to 'the sequel of the adventure', which furthers the link between the two scenes, and thus clearly establishes Romeo's own foresight into the violence of the romance that is to unfold. These fears of rape or being discarded are evident throughout Juliet's dialogue, "Thou mayst prove false. At lover's perjuries, / They say, Jove laughs," (l. 91–93). This displays the sense of self-protection that is constantly reinforced (l. 105, 111, 118, 143, 150) not just in this scene but also in the even more risk-filled (for her) Act III, Scene V after they have consummated the marriage and Romeo is about to leave for Mantua.

It is obvious from the outset that sexuality is constantly upon the minds of the characters within the play – bawdy puns, who to marry, and the rest. Violence affects all the characters in the play and the tension in the story is set around the violence of the two warring households. Nonetheless, as can be seen, separation between violence and sexuality is not often made. Even in the most idealistic situations violent themes and violent treatments underlie romantic verse.

And to sink in it, should you burden love – / Too great oppression for a tender thing.

Works Cited

Shakespeare, W. 1980. *Romeo and Juliet.* Ed. by Brian Gibbons, Singapore: Arden Shakespeare.

Watson, R.N. 2005. "Wherefore Art Thou Tereu? Juliet and the Legacy of Rape". *Renaissance Quarterly,* 58.1: 127–56.

LINES

Daniel Zachary Jones

Lines horizontal like blinds –

Each one crowds the vision

Each focuses the eye

Narrows thought

Brings up what you breathe,

And leaves

Parcels of what is there,

Freed for the minds creation.

PAUL'S GLASS CAGE

Hannah Lee

INT. GLASSHOUSE – DAY

Flitting around the ceiling of a large glasshouse is a panicked bird trying to find a way out. Every now and then it rams its body against the glass, and while this is a futile attempt to escape, it doesn't seem to want to stop.

FADE TO:

INT. GLASSHOUSE – DAY

This time we look down on the exotic flowers and ferns that fill the glasshouse. With abundant colour and beauty, the glasshouse is clearly a product of someone's hard work and care.

On a small square of grass, bordered by tiled paths, there is an elegant white table with two matching chairs. Sitting in one the chairs is SONYA, smoking a cigarette in her pyjamas. She is dark, thin and beautiful, but simultaneously unclean, unkempt and coarse. She shakes a hand through her long, brown, unwashed hair and pretends not to notice PAUL walking toward her in his pyjamas.

PAUL

You want the plants to die too?

SONYA ignores PAUL. PAUL sits in the other chair.

SONYA

Where were you?

PAUL

I was picking out all the dead fish
in the pond over there.

He places three dead, wet goldfish onto the table.

SONYA
(unfeelingly)
I wonder why they're dying.

PAUL

It might be your cigarette smoke.

SONYA

Don't be stupid.

She deliberately blows smoke over the dead fish. PAUL sees this as a
personal stab at him.

PAUL

You're going to get lung cancer
if you don't quit soon.

SONYA
I don't care.

PAUL
You should. Or at least do it
in or more ventilated space.

SONYA
Leave me alone.

There is an uncomfortable silence, save for the sound of a bird somewhere in the glasshouse.

PAUL
(quickly trying to lighten the mood)
That bird still in here?
It flew in almost a week ago.
I've given up trying to
catch it. No point. It'll
probably die soon anyway.

The bird lands on the table. Dead. SONYA rolls her eyes. PAUL, initially shocked and slightly disturbed by the dead bird, weakly tries to retain his light-heartedness.

PAUL
Ha. What I tell you?
I knew it'd be any day now.

SONYA
(cutting in)
What do you want?!

                          PAUL
                      (defensively)
                          What?

                          SONYA
                       (defeated)
                   What do you want?

PAUL considers the question, turning it over in his head. He gathers enough
courage to face SONYA and drops the cheerful act.

                          PAUL
                    I want new fish.

SONYA eyes him curiously. While PAUL speaks, SONYA smokes her
cigarette to the very end and crushes it on the table.

                          PAUL
              That's right. I want new fish.
          And I want a self-watering system in here
                 so I don't have to do it.
                          Yeah …
                 Now that I think about it
                    I want more time
              to relax. I want to just sit down and read
              a book once in a while, you know?
          I want to go on holiday and travel. Travel!
                     See the world.
          I want to make new friends and speak
          a different language. Something crazy
                     like Hebrew.
                  I want to be smart.

> Not that I think I'm dumb, but
> I want to learn more. I want to
> go to night school.

SONYA raises her eyebrows as she riffles through a packet of cigarettes. She taps the packet on the bottom to try and force the cigarettes out. PAUL is slightly put off by her lack of attention to him but he doesn't stop for a second.

PAUL
I want to know enough about something
to teach it.
I want to lecture someone about something
and not feel like a total ass.
I want to have an intelligent conversation
with people at a party.

PAUL clicks his fingers loudly as if an idea has struck him.

PAUL
More parties. I want to go to more parties.
I want to HOLD more parties. Invite all
my new friends from all over the world.
Friends from night school,
who can speak Hebrew.
I want people to look at me a certain way too.
But without knowing it. I want respect.
Admiration and ...
I want abs!

SONYA
(disbelievingly with a cigarette dangling

out of her mouth)
Abs?

PAUL
(with solid certainty)
Abs.
I want to be in better shape.
But without trying.
I want to be one of those old men
who you look at and think,
"that guy's gone to the gym".

SONYA
(quietly to herself)
Good luck.

PAUL
I want to live till I'm a hundred so that
when people ask, how old are you?
I can say, a century.
I want to give people my hundred
year old wisdom.
I want to die having had sex with
a wide range of women from different
nationalities.
European, Asian, Hispanic ...

SONYA
(getting out of her chair)
Goodbye Paul.

PAUL
What?!

SONYA starts walking away from the table. PAUL, confused as to what he
has done wrong, follows SONYA who walks with her arms crossed.

PAUL
You asked me what I want,
and I'm telling you.
I mean, I've still got more
to say but now I don't know
what you want to hear.
(not knowing how to ease SONYA'S
temper)
I mean, what do you want?

SONYA turns around and walks toward PAUL. She picks up a nearby pot
and smashes it on a tiled pathway. PAUL jumps at this sudden act of rage.

PAUL
WHAT THE FUCK?!

SONYA picks up another one and smashes it.

PAUL
What are you doing?

SONYA moves to a row of delicate flowers and stands dangerously close
to them.

PAUL
(sensing her next move)

Don't.

SONYA pulls one out so that its tiny roots are showing.

                              PAUL
                 Have you gone absolutely insane?!

SONYA begins to pull them out by handfuls. PAUL rushes to her and grabs her wrists.

                              PAUL
                 WHAT IS WRONG WITH YOU?!

SONYA spits in his face, he loosens his grip and she storms off, tipping pot plants and destroying everything in her reach. As she walks determinedly through the greenhouse, pulling apart plants and smashing pots, she begins to cough occasionally.

Having wiped spit from his face, PAUL tries to find SONYA. He follows her path of destruction, fuming with anger.

SONYA continues, coughing more violently as she continues damaging the plants with a cigarette in hand.

PAUL'S feet quickly pace along a tiled pathway strewn with dirt and broken pot pieces.

SONYA'S feet kick over neatly lined pots.

PAUL pushes back ferns to round a corner, and sees a car tyre hurled into what was once a neat row of plants. He looks a little confused as to how that got there but he continues.

SONYA turns over a large tray full of freshly sewn seeds and turns to run straight into the arms of PAUL. Both of them are breathing heavily. They don't say anything for a while. The plants still standing in the background slowly begin to decay - curling into colours of brown and black.

PAUL looks into SONYA'S eyes. They are watering. Her face is pale, her hair matted with sweat.

> PAUL
> What is the matter with you?

> SONYA
> I'm scared.

> PAUL
> Of what?

> SONYA
> Hold me.

> PAUL
> (frightened)
> I am holding you.

Orange lights flicker on SONYA'S face. PAUL looks outside and can only see flames licking the glasshouse. He cannot believe what he is seeing. He slowly lowers SONYA to the ground, still holding her tightly. She begins coughing violently. PAUL is shaken by how suddenly things have gone wrong.

> SONYA
> I wanted new fish.

(she laughs at how silly it sounds)
It's stupid but I really did.
And I wanted a self-watering system in there
so I didn't have to do it.
I wanted more time
to relax, you know?
I wanted to just sit down in there
and read
a book once in a while.

The following words said by SONYA overlap images of the past.

CROSS FADE TO:

EXT. ESTATE ON WHICH THE GREENHOUSE IS – DAY

… a time when both SONYA and PAUL were locking up the greenhouse on a foggy morning. They are both dressed nicely for a long drive back to college where they can start their studies again after a weekend away. PAUL extends his hand and SONYA takes it. They walk up a hill on which SONYA'S parents stand. Her father telling them to hurry.

EXT. SONYA'S HOUSE – DAY

PAUL and SONYA say goodbye to her parents and get in a car that's loaded with their luggage in the back.

SONYA (V.O.)
I wanted to go on holiday and travel.
See the world.
I wanted to make new friends and speak
a different language. Something crazy

like Hebrew.
(she laughs painfully)
I wanted to be smart.
Not that I think I'm dumb, but
I wanted to learn more. I wanted to
go to night school or something.
I wanted to know enough about something
to teach it.
I wanted to lecture someone about something
and not feel like a total ass.

INT. CAR – DAY

PAUL and SONYA drive down a foggy road. SONYA takes out a cigarette and lights it.

PAUL
You're going to get lung cancer
if you don't quit soon.

SONYA
(not really listening)
I don't care.

PAUL
You should.
(jokingly)
Or at least do it
in or more ventilated space.

PAUL opens a window.

SONYA
(playfully)
Leave me alone.

PAUL
(pretending to preach)
I'm telling you. You're
going to get lung cancer.

SONYA laughs and accidentally coughs.

PAUL
Ha. What I tell you?
I knew it'd be any day now.

SONYA clears her throat, repositions her arm against the window sill and
rolls her eyes. A bird can be heard in the background.

PAUL
What?

SONYA continues smoking and looking out the window.

PAUL
What, are you angry with me?
...
Oh come on.

PAUL tries to tickle SONYA. SONYA pushes him away pretending to be
mad, but she is smiling.

PAUL stops the car. He looks into her eyes with over-exaggerated sincerity.

PAUL

I don't know what you want me to

say anymore.

SONYA smirks while looking down at her feet. She hates feeling sentimental because she's always hated couples who show affection openly. But she can't help looking up at PAUL and smiling. The shape of a semi-trailer becomes increasingly discernible through fog over SONYA'S shoulder. It hits their car instantly before PAUL can finish his sentence.

PAUL

What do you want –

OVER BLACK

SONYA (V.O.)

I wanted to live till I was a hundred so that

when people asked, how old are you?

I could say, a century.

I wanted to give people my hundred

year old wisdom.

INT. GLASSHOUSE – NIGHT

PAUL lies in a bed of decayed grass. Everything around him has died and a cold moonlight floods the dead forest in its greenhouse enclosure. He looks outside. SONYA is sitting on the grass outside smoking a cigarette and looking up at the moon. He digs his hands into the black soil. The broken pots remain untouched. SONYA'S cigarette smoke curls up into the night sky and disappears into the clear and crisp air.

CHAIN OF FOOLS

Angela Rossi

———

The trees that courted the wind,

the wind that ruffled feathers,

the feathers that dusted knowledge,

the knowledge that turned true,

the truth that charmed chaos,

the chaos that spoiled youths,

the youth that spoke out,

the outspoken that sent shivers,

the shivers that transfigured into tremors,

the tremors that swayed the trees that courted the wind who dances with the leaves and falls into the eaves of above.

UNTITLED

Kate Farrell

The trees shed their coats –

Yellow flakes, peeled

From the painted sky

Light and leaf fluttered down

Into guttermush.

Corner house, Sold sign

Exclamation marked and empty.

A piano stands quietly inside,

Awaiting fresh hands

A truck approaches,

Ironing out the road

Its wheels wended.

Furniture moves in then

An owner,

Invisible like cold,

No more neighbour than

The last, yet soft notes fall

Over the fence,

His fingers leaking music

On the keys.

We donned our coats

And took rakes to

Push and pull

Beneath the naked trees.

ANNIE'S

Will Atkinson

I'd gone through half a bottle of the cooking sherry from the back of the pantry when I started to feel sleepy. The word count at the bottom of my screen had moved in fits all day, only to reduce in turn by revision. At one point I had shouted into a telephone, but the reason why now evaded me and I felt slightly guilty for it. I had an interest in collecting euphemisms for being struck by wordlessness. One was appropriate for this case. It was like trying to strain shit through a sock.

At three o'clock I had told myself that the sherry would shift it. But within an hour of pouring the first sickly glass, my head was unmistakably heading deskward, blurringly surveying my red laminex domain. It's hard to describe exactly what happens at the point of falling asleep, but this time I was aware of every moment of the process, and it felt, as far as I can remember, as if a hand was pulling me upwards with a sudden jerk as soon as my eyes had closed.

***

And then my eyes opened. In front of me was a red velvet hanging, of such an intense hue that it consumed my entire field of vision. I wheeled around, my eyes adjusting to the light of a room lit entirely with candles. It was a long, smoky space, a cross between an art-nouveau boudoir and a bad restaurant owned by a successful doctor or lawyer in order to keep the wife occupied. On a red-buttoned leather banquette sat a short, fat man in a fine double-breasted suit. He had gold-framed glasses, which periodically slid down to the end of his sweat drenched nose. In a single movement, he would push them back up and smooth down his slicked hair, exhaling noisily through his mouth.

The table was covered with piles of receipts and invoices, which the man was arranging into piles. I made to walk towards him, but as soon as the thought had entered my head, he held a hand up to stop me.

Wait.

I froze, as if on cue. The man's voice was high pitched and emphatic, with the potential for petulance hiding behind every word. I had read somewhere that people were able to control the direction of their dreams with enough practice. A creature of my own admittedly dull imagining had stopped me short, who on first glance resembled both a greyhound track owner and a state government minister. There was something in what I'd read that said that you couldn't properly read in a dream, too. I picked up a heavy, sequinned menu from a footstool to my right. The cover read "Annie's". A review thoughtfully pasted on the inner cover profiled its signature dish. Confit of ocean trout.

There was a hearty thwack as the man in the suit unceremoniously dropped a large pile of papers onto the floor beside his feet. With effort, he slowly turned his body toward mine, and as his eyes met mine, I swore I caught a violent flash of red, which dissipated as I turned to his mouth, which wore a lizard grin.

Please, forgive me for keeping you waiting, he said with exaggerated politeness. Have a seat.

My body involuntarily jerked forwards, and I took a seat at the other end of the banquette. The piles of invoices were neatly arranged on the tabletop.

He looked at me, smiled, and dropping his gaze, hurled his arm across the table, sending them flying onto the carpet. The restaurant – well, whatever it was – was quite empty. I didn't bat an eyelid.

It's no fun playing the accountant, Ian. Drink?

Yes, I said. A gin and tonic. He reached into his jacket, extracted a tumbler, and snapped a thumb over it. Something approximating the look of a gin and tonic appeared in the glass, and throwing caution to the wind, I took a small sip. Smooth. The flavours – all fifteen or so of them – were in perfect harmony. The gin and tonic *ne plus ultra*.

I'm the Devil, by the by.

My name is Ian, I replied.

I know.

He smiled with the calm benevolence of someone conversing with the slightly retarded. The casualness with which my companion revealed that he was the Prince of Darkness did much to calm me. I laughed, then stopped, wondering what I was laughing about.

I recommend the parsnip fries with the mayonnaise aioli.

They appeared on the table with a quiet click of the bowl on the table, and my new companion again reached into the depths of his suit and emerged with a mint julep. The crushed mint smelled divine, cutting across the citrus of the elaborately carved lemon peel sitting atop my drink. He took several chips, dipped them, and brought them to his mouth, one-by-one. He chewed noisily as his eyes caught mine, staring deeply into them.

What am I doing here? I asked. He continued chewing, and gestured to the bowl. I hesitated, and took a chip, nibbling at it carefully. It was delicious, salty, with a firm but yielding texture. The Devil wiped his hands on his lapels and readjusted his glasses.

It's in the contract, he said offhandedly. I have at least one meal with every mortal being before they die. Go on, try the aioli, it's subtle enough not to make your breath stink.

Feeling almost compelled, I scooped an honest amount of aioli on another chip, and munched thoughtfully.

When I say at least one, it doesn't mean that I don't have repeat diners. Depends on whether they're good company. I've had some doozies in my time, let me tell you.

Like who? I half-expected a roll call of history's evilest.

You'd be surprised, he replied. Ordinary people – people who are at least honest about what they enjoy. You know, I've had decades of conversation with certain model train enthusiasts.

The Devil, or the perspiring man in front of me who claimed to be him, was about as far removed from the fallen angel I'd heard about. I couldn't see his fat, slightly feminine hands caught amidst any great intrigue. He seemed a surburbanite desperately trying to be urbane; the type of man you might have seen having his morning coffee in a village plaza, holding forth and laying out plans for a wine bar next to the pharmacy. I looked up again, and saw he held my gaze.

I'm not quite what you expected, am I?

His lips had not moved when he said it, but his voice was clear in my ears and his eyes flashed. I managed a weak smile, which faded rapidly. Almost brusquely, he pushed the bowl of chips towards me. I took them. He spoke again, quite wearily.

I've existed under a cloud of unwarranted suspicion on your world for many years. But I'm one necessary part of a whole. It's an intricate balancing act, Ian. I'm afraid you won't get quite as fine a meal with my counterpart.

The Devil lay back on the banquette and folded his arms magisterially over his stomach. His fingers, covered in heavy gold rings, tapped out a thoughtful rhythm on the buttons of his suit.

But now to the wine. This is a red I get in bulk from an excellent supplier. Don't worry about it being a cleanskin. I think you'll be surprised.

The half-finished gin and tonic disappeared from my hands, and in front of me was a beautiful crystal wine stem, with the capacity of a small bucket. He held a bottle over it, and it was soon filled with red so rich and dark it overwhelmed even the restaurant's décor. Pouring himself a glass, he took it, snuffled at it, and chewed it around his mouth, making a soft murmur of deep contentment.

And to dinner.

A menu appeared before me. His eyes brightened and his head bobbed enthusiastically as I scanned the daily specials. I was quietly aware of becoming excruciatingly hungry. After a short while, he gently lifted the menu from my grip.

I think we'll have the dinner menu #2.

Over the time I sat at that table – and I forgot how long it was – I ate some of the finest food ever plated. I had to restrain myself from emitting small orgasmic grunts as I wrestled with the courses, culminating in a rack of lamb so perfectly done that the only trace left behind was a few sinew-covered bones and a pink juice at the bottom of my plate. The only misstep, I felt, was a slightly too tough poached pear with my cassata at dessert, but the Devil was quick to outline the difficulties with the season's pear yield in careful detail.

We talked between mouthfuls, mostly about food, and his entire body shook with excitement when discussing a certain pâté, or the different methods of roasting a potato. He came across as a slightly excitable uncle, a vain man given to fluttering hand gestures, punctuated by charming moments of coarseness.

Vegans, he said at one point, are haters of freedom. Do them a favour and run them over.

I giggled in appreciation.

He reminded me of a man with a singular interest that he pursued wholly, the type that would talk over you if at any time you tried to introduce another topic of conversation. Yet beneath it all, there was something inexpressible about him, something that he seemed to be holding back.

Ian.

I heard his voice through the fog, extending my name in a long drawl. He had begun to swirl his whisky around a heavy tumbler, and from the downturned corners of his mouth I could sense he was a little drunk. The food itself sat heavily in me – I think we had been eating for hours, even days – and I gladly settled it with a small port.

Tell me. About yourself.

Now, a question like that generally leads to an immediate cessation in interesting conversation, for the simple fact that at my age I've nothing interesting to relate. I am currently unemployed. My parents were quite correct, in hindsight, about that Arts degree. Nevertheless, I began to rattle off the usual roll-call of twenty-one year old insecurities and views held extremely, at which he nodded at with arms folded, occasionally looking at the ceiling.

Even the painful mention of that girl I was interested in running off with and the guy from the café with the jeans so tight you could see in sharp relief the veins on his balls elicited nothing more than a quiet snort. With visible force he held up a hand when I brought up my plans to visit Morocco.

He had changed – his face seemed suddenly leaner, with a distinct sneer cutting across his mouth instead of his usual reptilian grin. He placed his glasses on the table, looked up, and I could see his faint-red pupils glower.

Enough of this. To business.

In a soft murmur, he added: what do you desire?

What do I desire? I replied. Nothing. I'm full.

No, forget the dinner, you idiot. In life. Your greatest desires in life.

I sat back in my seat, flustered. I didn't really have any, besides those I didn't think polite to air to the Devil. Or my mother, who is an efficient yardstick to follow in unfamiliar situations.

I can't see into the future, he continued, but I have lived for years beyond mortal kin. I have traced the paths of humankind over the centuries, seeing empires rise and fall in the twinkling of an eye. I have often taken part. A young man of your stature surely desires something – and I can give it to you. Knowledge that transcends time and space. Power, wealth, the ability to read men's minds, to find minerals hidden deep in the earth. What do you desire?

I stopped to consider. The Devil, quite drunken, was giving a bravura performance. The restaurant seemed to grow darker with his every word, and he seemed to increase in size. It was scintillating. I was determined to not reduce the intensity of the situation.

Sir, I began. After such a meal, I'm at a risk of falling flat here with my greatest desire.

Never, he replied, his face rounding out to its previous, amiable self. His eyes transformed into an indistinct blue. In fact, I was thinking we could go into partnership.

Partnership! That put another spin on things. Oh, the long lunches we would have, my Horned Prince of Misrule and I! The practicalities of any potential venture were of no concern. He put a heavy leather case on the table, opened it, and brought out a blank sheet of paper and a fountain pen. In a looping hand, he wrote out a contract in maroon ink, pausing with a blot as I fought with the idea that I was potentially misinterpreting the offer.

A door had opened to the possibilities of our relationship. Almost perfectly formed, I saw a plan emerge crystalline and distinct into my mind.

Satan, I quivered.

Yes? His voice betrayed the quietest hint of impatience.

Let's open a chain of Annie's restaurants. We'll take this shit global. All over the place. In airports. In every major city. Can you imagine the celebrities we'd pull? The reviews we'd get. A television spin-off. The dining experience to beat every dining experience. Can we resurrect Frank Sinatra? He'll perform. Nightly.

As I spoke with chemically enhanced enthusiasm, a curious pall fell over the Devil's eyes. He snapped on the cap of his pen, which had been hungrily poised above the contract. With difficulty, he managed a slow, twitchy smile, but his eyes remained hard, and fixed on mine. Worldlessly, he looked me up and down, gathered his contract, and snapped shut his expensive brief. He stood up, saluted me, turned quickly and left the restaurant, slamming the door behind him.

I don't quite have the words to explain what happened next, but before my eyes the restaurant began to decay. The rich hangings turned to ash, the leather cracked and split, pushing out tufts of foam, and the carpet became thick with dust. Mirrors became spotted, reflecting no longer a rich red, but a grey that sat faintly in the darkening room. The plates on the table in front of me, covered with scraps, decayed in front of my eyes, and enormous rats descended from the ceiling to fight over the carbonised remains.

***

I woke with an involuntary shriek, knocking a half-empty bottle of cooking sherry to the floor, where it began to glug out its sticky remnants across the lino. In front of me was a small card, with nothing more on its front but a slightly charred pentagram. Stuck on the back was a small mint. "With compliments". There was a number. I haven't called it yet.

AND THE WALL CAME TUMBLING DOWN

NATO's Place in a Post-Cold War World

Joanna Twartz

———

The North Atlantic Treaty Organization (NATO) was founded to be a collective defence mechanism for the United States of America and its European allies in the face of the growing Soviet threat during the Cold War (Carlson 2007). However, massive changes have occurred within NATO (Carlson 2007), which have resulted from the dissolution of the Soviet Union. Two years after the end of the Cold War, the prospects for long-term development remained unclear and there was no real consensus among the member states as to the place and role of the alliances after the war (Davydov 1997). NATO was not expected to reform internally because it no longer served its purpose (Gehrcke 2008). Yet, twenty years later, the organisation is still alive and well. How has NATO changed since the end of the Cold War so that it is still relevant today? And what were the causes for these changes? This essay argues that NATO has continued to exist because it is no longer a collective defence alliance purely aimed at protecting the North Atlantic states from the Soviet empire. Instead, NATO has adopted three new objectives that have changed the structures of the alliances. First, NATO has pushed its way in to Eastern Europe as a way of keeping Russia at bay, which is an adaption of its original purpose of stopping the

———

spread of the Soviet Union. Secondly, NATO now spends considerable effort spreading democracy around the world as a way of ensuring stability. Lastly, NATO continues to operate as a collective defence organisation but what they defend has changed: moving away from a purely European to a worldwide focus along with assisting in the collective security of the world. NATO has been forced to change and continues to exist because it adapted to the new unilateral world system. It continues to fulfil its original purpose, albeit in a slightly amended fashion and by adopting new principles.

Containing Russia

Alliances are formed either by balancing or bandwagoning (Walt 1985). In response to a perceived threat, a state will either form an alliance with the offender's enemy in an attempt to create a balance of power, or join the offender in an attempt to avoid any more action being taken against them. The latter phenomenon is known as bandwagoning (Walt 1985). Until the end of the Cold War, the tendency of alliances in the international system was to balance the power. This can be seen from the bipolar world system that persisted throughout the nineteenth and twentieth centuries (Walt 1985).

NATO's original purpose was to balance the Soviet Union's power at a time when its empire stretched from Eastern Germany to Mongolia, Afghanistan to Vietnam and beyond (Traill 2009). Among NATO's twelve original members were the most powerful democracies on the planet (Daalder & Goldgeier 2006). In contrast, at the end of the Cold War, moves were made to extend membership to eastern and central European states, particularly those that were part of the Soviet bloc. This shift was seen as contrary to Russia's national interest (Davydov 1997). By 2004, membership had been extended to another twelve eastern and central European states, and by 2009, membership of NATO was at twenty-six (NATO, 2010a). The gradual inclusion of eastern and central Europe by NATO was a geopolitical process designed to eradicate the long-standing division of Europe caused by the Cold War (Kuus 2007). Except the frightening effect this had on Russia was no accident. After signing the *Charter for American–Russian Friendship and Cooperation* in 1992, Russia began to reduce her nuclear arsenal as per their agreement. NATO took this opportunity to expand across eastern and central Europe (Legvold 2007). Russia's weakness and lack of ability to use deterrence in the early 1990s was encouragement for the United States to solidify her standing as the last remaining superpower through enlarging NATO (Mearsheimer 2001).

NATO had created a seemingly unified European empire, creeping ever closer to Russia, encroaching on what had once been Russia's safety zone. This was a direct threat to Russia's national interest (Ambrosio 2005), as the approach of the world's largest military bloc to her borders placed strain on the Russian military budget. Furthermore, it jeopardised Russia's military reform and intensified nationalist and anti-reformist movements within the country (Davydov 1997). In response, Russia's president, Boris Yeltsin, denounced the United States' move into the former Soviet Bloc countries claiming that the United Nations should grant Russia special powers to govern over the region (Legvold 2007a), while still retaining membership on the Security Council. This was done in an attempt to balance the new hegemon and defend her neighbours, but was ultimately of no use in preventing the unilateral system from emerging (Legvold 2007). NATO had already achieved its new goal of preventing Russia becoming a superpower and keeping her at bay within her borders. A move by eastern and central European states to bandwagon with the US superpower made this possible because it enabled a solidification of the new unilateral world order.

Projecting Democracy

Under the liberalist paradigm, "promoting freedom will produce peace" (Doyle 1986). At the centre of the liberal world is the promotion of democracy, through basic human rights, a people's government, the right to own property and an open market. This in turn will lead to security since democratic states are far less likely to go to war with other democratic states (Dunne 2008).

After years of war, all NATO members signed the *Rome Declaration of Peace and Cooperation* (NATO 2010). Whilst the purpose of the alliance during the Cold War was collective defence (Carlson 2007), the declaration emphasised the importance of stability in Europe (NATO 2010). Decision-makers collectively agreed that democracy in eastern and central Europe was the key stability and security (Gheciu 2005). By bringing eastern and central European states into a realm of liberal ideals, NATO invested in constructing domestic democratic choices for eastern and central European states and shaping legal and institutional arrangements for the post-communist bloc countries (Gheciu 2005). NATO now aimed for the protection and promotion of its liberal and democratic values. This was a new internal dimension to the alliance, which was only allowed to flourish once the external threat from the Soviet Union had diminished (Gheciu 2005). NATO aimed to foster a sense of community and cooperative security emanating from the core states to eastern and central European states (Adler 2008). In addition, it aimed to protect the "European value" of democracy and liberalism (Kuus 2007) to ensure stability.

NATO also became a forum for eastern and central European states to communicate with the only remaining world superpower (Gheciu 2005) and also became a model for the new Economic Commission for Europe (ECE) organisations that began to emerge (Bailes et al. 2007). Integration with the new world order was thought to create stability and security, consistent with liberal ideas.

The model of projecting democracy into the ex-Soviet space was not without problems. Eastern and central European states were not perfect members of

NATO, as they were still new to the notion of democracy. Their populations view the new alliance in a different way. This created some unsolvable problems between the NATO core and new members (Soloch 2009). The inclusion of some eastern and central European states additionally created a divide between those who were invited to the club and those poorer states who did not meet the criteria to join either NATO or the European Union (Stent 2007). Creating stability by spreading democracy is a slow process and has many obstacles along the way.

The nature and dynamics of this exercise of power were very different from those of the prevailing conception of coercion used toward Russia (Gheciu 2005). NATO found it difficult to reconcile its move in to ECE as a stability program or as a deterrence strategy against Russia (Betts 2009). NATO was and is still torn between offensive moves against Russia and maintaining its "club for democracies" (Betts 2009). While NATO does have a renewed mandate to project democracy into Europe, this always comes second to militarily defending its members.

Collective Defence and Collective Security

Collective defence differs from the "all for one and one for all" notion of collective security since it is a balance of power, not an universal community; an organised rivalry (Miller 2001). Essentially, collective security protects its members from a threat from within the collective, whereas collective defence protects its members from an external threat. This has the benefit of a combined front to those outside, as well as being able to share the burden of costs through economies of scale (Hartley 2006). NATO was set up as a collective defence organisation, whereas the United Nations endeavoured to espouse the universality required for collective security (Miller 2001). Nevertheless, during the Cold War, when bipolarity reigned supreme, regional and bloc security measures often overruled the collective security of the United Nations (Miller 2001). In the post-Cold War era, whilst the notion of collective security seemed to be in working order, the United Nations do not have the instruments to ensure security throughout the world. The United Nations has more than once asked NATO to supply armed forces and ensure security throughout the world (Miller 2001).

Along with becoming involved with the collective security of the world at large, NATO still operates as a collective defence mechanism. With the collapse of the Soviet Union, NATO states no longer faced "the old threat of massive attack" from the east (NATO 2010). However, it was recognised that there may still be risks in the future and that members needed to remain at the ready to deal with them as they arose. Thus, the collective defence nature of the alliance was retained (NATO 2010). In the process, NATO has endeavoured to maintain its trans-Atlantic interests (Hendrickson 2007) whilst also becoming the dominant military and political force in Europe (Caldwell 2007).

Nonetheless, since the end of the Cold War several problems have arisen, which prevent collective defence from occurring the way it was envisioned. Eastern and central European states are new to the democratic realm and are still adjusting to the notion of their states being secure, so they do not have the infrastructure to contribute to collective security (Kuus 2007). Likewise, there have been multiple informal alliances evolve worldwide which are outside the traditional sphere of influence of NATO, not least of which is the Russia–China alliance, threatening the power of NATO and stability in Europe (Ambrosio 2005).

NATO has attempted to overcome these problems by expanding its sphere of influence and consequently restructuring its armed forces. NATO has expanded its sphere of influence beyond its traditional sphere in response to threats moving from outside the traditional North Atlantic sphere (Ambrosio 2005) and in 2002 approved a package that included the ability to respond to out-of-area threats (NATO 2010). This was done through a program of cooperative security (Adler 2008) incorporating democracies worldwide. Given that the new European member states did not necessarily have the resources to contribute to NATO the way the core did, other non-member states who share the same democratic and liberal ideas as NATO have been called in to fulfil this responsibility (Daadler & Goldgeier 2006), creating the economies of scale required for collective defence. These states include Australia, Brazil, India, Japan, New Zealand, South Africa and South Korea (Daadler & Goldgeier 2006). Post-Cold War there was a distinct increase in the number of actions taken by this new "coalition of the willing" (Fang & Ramsay 2010). It was the demise of the *Warsaw Pact* that led to the agreement to operate worldwide (Lagoa & Piella 2010).

Two missions that NATO has been involved with since the end of the Cold War show how it has begun to operate on both collective defence and collective security levels. NATO provided strategic airlift and training to the African Union in the Sudan in 2005 (NATO 2010). This was a defence mechanism, as the control of the Sudanese crisis would lead to the security of resources for NATO members. On the other hand, during the Yugoslavian crisis of the early 1990s, NATO forces acted as "an agent of UN police power" (Miller 2001). Whilst the action taken against Milošević could be seen as collective defence on NATO's part, the action was not taken until the United Nations Security Council requested their assistance. At this point the provision of NATO forces became part of a universal action to secure Yugoslavia, a result of the collective security system that had been set up by the United Nations (Miller 2001).

The introduction of new actors to the coalition required a homogenisation of the military forces available to NATO, a renewed command structure and new planning processes and with a new framework of relationships with the new non-member allies (Lagoa & Piella 2010). This was all undertaken in order to ensure the alliance could operate to its greatest potential to ensure the safety of not just the members, but also the non-member states that helped it.

Whilst it may not seem like a big change, the end of the Cold War turned NATO's collective defence exercises from the defence of twelve states in western Europe and North America, towards the defence of democracy worldwide and the assistance of security for the entire world. This is effectively a show of power that NATO is not only the dominant military force in Europe, but now also worldwide and is willing to ensure the protection of its members and its values worldwide. Threats from outside the alliance still exist, although NATO is now capable of dealing with any attack from outside any one of its members or informal allies, therefore proving its fundamental basis of collective defence and providing collective security.

Conclusion

NATO has undergone massive changes since 1991. The disappearance of its sole purpose to balance the power of the Soviet Union, led to these changes. After some time of confusion as to NATO's place in the post-Cold War world, NATO has now solidified its role. This has come about because the decision-makers within the alliance collectively agreed to change the aim of the alliance. Rather than just purely balance the Soviet Union's power, NATO took on three new roles. Firstly, containing Russia within her borders to prevent a repeat of the Soviet Union expansion in to Eastern Europe. Moreover, spreading democracy throughout eastern and central Europe to encourage stability and security in a unified Europe. Ultimately, turning their collective defence focus to protecting democratic values and liberty throughout the world and ensuring the security of all nations, instead of focusing solely on Europe. NATO has overcome an inability to function or reform and by changing its mandate has managed to change the way it functions in the world. It has solidified its place as a force to be reckoned with in the new unilateral, post-Cold War world.

Works Cited

Adler, E. 2008. "The Spread of Security Communities: Communities of Practice, Self-Restraint, and NATO's Post-Cold War Transformation". *European Journal of International Relations*, Vol. 14, No. 2: 195–230.

Ambrosio, T. 2005. *Challenging America's Global Preeminence: Russia's Quest for Multipolarity*. Aldershot, Hampshire, UK: Ashgate Publishing.

Bailes, A., Baranovsky, V. & Dunay, P. 2007. "Regional Security Cooperation in the Former Soviet Area". *Stockholm International Peace Research Institute Yearbook*, Vol. 2007.

Betts, R. 2009. "The Three Faces of NATO". *The National Interest*, No. 100: 31–38.

Caldwell, L. 2007. "Russian Concepts of National Security". In *Russian Foreign Policy in the Twenty-First Century and the Shadow of the Past*, pp 279–342. Ed. by R. Legvold, New York: Columbia University Press.

Carlson, B. 2007. "Examining the Process of Regime Change in the North Atlantic Treaty Organization: The Divide Between Rhetoric and Reality". *Dissertation Abstracts International, A: The Humanities and Social Sciences*, Vol. 67, No. 9: 35–75.

Daalder, I. & Goldgeier, J. 2006. "Global NATO". *Foreign Affairs*, Vol. 85, No. 5: 105–13.

Davydov, Y. 1997. "Russian Security and East-Central Europe". In *Russia and Europe: The Emerging Security Agenda*, pp 368–85. Ed. by V. Baranovsky, Oxford: Oxford University Press.

Doyle, M. 1986. "Liberalism and World Politics". *American Political Science Review*, Vol. 80, No. 4: 1151–69.

Dunne, T. 2008. "Liberalism". In *The Globalization of World Politics: An Introduction to International Relations*, pp 108–123. Ed. by Baylis, J., Smith, S. & Owens, P., 4th ed., Oxford: Oxford University Press.

Fang, S. & Ramsay, K. 2010. "Outside Option and Burden Sharing in Nonbinding Alliances". *Political Research Quarterly*, Vol. 63, No. 1: 188–202.

Gehrcke, W. 2008. "NATO's Identity Crisis". *WeltTrends*, No. 60: 115–18.

Ghecui, A. 2005. *NATO in the 'New Europe': The Politics of International Socialization After the Cold War*. Stanford: Stanford University Press.

Hartley, K. 2006. "Defence Industrial Policy in a Military Alliance". *Journal of Peace Research*, Vol. 43, No. 4: 473–89.

Hendrickson, R. 2007. "The Miscalculation of NATO's Death", *Parameters*, Vol. 37, No. 1: 98–114.

Kuus, M. 2007. *Geopolitics Reframed*, New York: Palgrave Macmillan.

Lagoa, E. & Piella, G. 2010. "NATO's Military Transformation: A Vision From Spain", *UNISCI Discussion Papers*, No. 22: 188–99.

Legvold, R., 2007, "Russian Foreign Policy During Period of Great State Transformation" in *Russian Foreign Policy in the Twenty-first Century and the Shadow of the Past*, pp 77–144. Ed. by R. Legvold, New York: Columbia University Press.

Legvold, R. (ed), 2007. *Russian Foreign Policy in the Twenty-First Century and the Shadow of the Past.* New York: Columbia University Press.

Mearsheimer, J. 2001. *The Tragedy of Great Power Politics,* New York: Norton.

Miller, L. 2001. "The Ideal and Reality of Collective Security". In *The Politics of Global Governance: International Organizations in an Interdependent World,* pp 171–201. Ed. by Diehl, P., 2nd ed. Boulder CO: Lynne Rienner Publishers.

NATO 2010. *North American Treaty Organization, NATO Mini.* Comm. Rome Declaration, 8th Nov 1991 [Online], Available: www.nato.int/docu/comm/49-95/c911108a.htm [15 April 2010].

Rieber, A. 2007. "How Persistent Are Persistent Factors?" In *Russian Foreign Policy in the Twenty-First Century and the Shadow of the Past,* pp 205–78. Ed. by R. Legvold, New York: Columbia University Press.

Soloch, K. 2009. "Central European Countries Torn Between European Solidarity and Atlantic Preference". *Politique etrangere,* No. 3: 541–51.

Stent, A. 2007. "Reluctant Europeans: Three Centuries of Russian Ambivalence Toward the West". In *Russian Foreign Policy in the Twenty-First Century and the Shadow of the Past,* pp 393–442. Ed. by R. Legvold, New York: Columbia University Press.

Traill, K. 2009. *Red Square Blues: A Beginner's Guide to the Decline and Fall of the Soviet Union.* Sydney: Harper Collins Publishers.

Walt, S. 1985. "Alliance Formation and the Balance of World Power". *International Security,* Vol. 9, No. 4: 1–43.

WE BEGIN IN WORDS

Sheila Monaghan

———

"We begin" (and end) "in words":

What I don't say is anything to hint at the nights,

days, strings of days – colliding into months

– careening into my ordered life, like the noisiest

thief I've never met, to snip away at moments and reduce me

to a figure swathed in shadows, at a perpetual 11pm.

I can't tell you about the saddest songs Google could provide,

seeping from my desk to cocoon me, as my back

– rigid against the itchy carpet – holds me in place upon the floor.

I did tell you once, that I had no secrets I'd never tell;

And I did tell you once, that we begin in words:

a constant act of creation. But what I didn't tell you once:

is that the creation is in your mind,

and my words suffice to do all the creating.

For me, I am contained by my omission.

For you, I am unconstrained; and so you are always waiting

for the next gardenbed of words.

THE DETECTIVES

Gabi Edelstein

———

It was a dark and stormy night at the manor. The wind was shaking the rafters and the rain was plummeting onto the rooftop of the Victorian house. The guests were relieved that it was finally time for tea; dinner was a long and arduous affair – far too many opinions at the dinner table as far as Miss Jane Marple was concerned. She did not care for the other guests, yabbering away about their recent jobs, "I solved that case" this and "I am such a great detective" that. The truth of the matter was: she was out of work. Their egotistic claptrap only served to point out that she hadn't had a case fall into her lap in over a year. Who wanted to hire a doddery old lady to solve a crime when a strapping young man like Philip Marlowe was up for grabs instead?

She and Poirot were sitting in the corner of the grand old parlour, sipping their tea and trying to make some sort of conversation. They had never gotten on, she thought he was a self-righteous Belgian and he thought she was a bird past her prime with an onset of Alzheimer's disease. But no matter, she'd rather sit with an overweight man with a too finely trimmed moustache than with the "hard-boiled" crew. Or with, even worse, Inspector Hound.

She looked around the decadent parlour. She had more pedestrian tastes. Well, her tastes constituted what she could afford. There were terribly high ceilings, and everything was in a green, red and gold colour scheme – it was as if Christmas had thrown up all over the room. It was a pity that the manor withstood space and time, she was destined to be trapped inside the horrid confines of her genre forever. She looked over at Poirot, everything in his room was probably ordered to the point of insanity. "What 'ave you been doing recently, *Madame*?" Poirot asked her. "Oh, well dear, you can not be so terribly busy all the time. I am taking a break at the moment" she offered in reply. "May I presume to ask what it is you are breaking from, *mon amie*?" he deigned to ask another question. "No, no, that is perfectly alright. I am currently taking a break from the world of criminal activity, actually. I am thinking of taking a trip to the Bahamas, in fact" she gave in answer "Ah, *le* Bahamas" he murmured, looking off to the other side of the room. Where was that Cordelia Gray character? She had wondered off with that Sam Spade man after dinner. Spade had returned but Gray did not. Curious. Was murder afoot?

Miss Marple sighed, was she eternally doomed to sit in this old house waiting for someone to write about her? She wasn't one for postmodern cynicism but she wasn't sure if she could take much more of this. She had been living with the hard-boilers for years but now they were becoming far too cosy; they smoked in the parlour, made jokes about her investigatory skills – did no one have any manners any more? And then there was Hound, shuffling around the room, picking up objects and putting them down again – as if trying to find some clue to the meaning of life!

She thought about poor Miss Cordelia, she was new around here. It still seemed that she didn't understand what was what in this house. Sherlock Holmes and Watson entered the dining room first (but they were away on "business", at the moment) and then came the cosies after them the hard-boiled and finally the parodies. But there seemed to be a resurgence of popularity in the hard-boilers genre – Miss Marple would rather eat her lace-trimmed hat then allow those dirty Americans into the dining room before her. Miss Marple felt some sympathy for poor Cordelia, her genre was just not defined enough – and thus she was forever doomed to sit with that imbecile, Hound.

Suddenly, the door to the parlour slammed open and in walked Sherlock, dripping wet, with Watson (as usual) trailing after him. They were home surprisingly early, and Sherlock looked as if he had just received quite a shock. "Elementary, elementary" she heard him mumble. Oh dear, it seemed that Sherlock was on the bottle again – everyone in the house knew that he was dying for a real adventure, something not so high-necked or dull. "Well, Holmes, how was it?" Marlowe piped up. "The mystery was solved in three days" provided Watson, "But I'm afraid Sherlock has come down with a cold of sorts". Miss Marple looked over at the hard-boilers and suddenly had eye contact with Spade. Could it be? Is Sherlock dying? Obviously he's not selling as many books as he used to, modern audiences just didn't want him anymore – they wanted sex and violence. This was not good for Miss Marple either – when Sherlock's stock was down hers was as well.

The sound of thunder ricocheted around the room and everything was silent once more. All of a sudden, a high-pitched scream was heard. No one moved. The detectives heard the loud pattering of footsteps suddenly coming in the direction of the room. Once more, the door was slammed open and in came the parlour maid. "Murder! Murder!" she screamed hysterically, sobbing in fits. "I knew it!" Hound interjected before anyone else could get a word in. Murder? Miss Marple wondered. It couldn't possibly be a subversion! Nothing this exciting has happened since 1947! She stood up quickly, trying not to crack any of her old bones. "Well?" she piped up, "Where is the body?" there was a harrumph of agreement throughout the room. The maid told everyone to follow her, and thus they began the trail through the house until they reached the library. Miss Marple was hardly surprised at the cliché; she'd seen this before in *The Body in the Library*! The first thing Miss Marple noticed as she walked into the room was the trail of crime-writing books. As they walked further in, the books became more recent. And there, on the floor lay Cordelia Gray, with a bottle of arsenic in one hand and a knife imbedded in her chest. "I 'ave seen this before in 1936, *Cards on le Table*" Poirot said, and there was appreciative (if not annoyed) hum throughout the room.

"I say" Sherlock said, "she is quite dead". "No she isn't", Hound replied. "Yes she is" "No she isn't" "Yes she is" "No she isn't". Was Miss Marple truly destined to spend the rest of her days hearing this ironic dribble?

All the detectives looked at each other in suspicion. This murder was too inane to be committed by someone who had seen it all. "I say, I say –" began Sherlock, again. "Oh shut it you old phoney, go play your violin!" burst in Marlowe. He was more antagonistic tonight than usual. Watson was about to speak in righteous indignation, but Poirot's voice beat him to it, "Really, *Monsieur* Marlowe, we 'ave all seen this before, surely it is not too 'ard to work out?". "Quieten up, Frenchman!" Spade erupted, "I am not French, I am from Belgium" Poirot explained, again. It was silent once more. What was the difference between Belgium and France anyway? "I am under the presumption that she was not selling the quota to be allowed into the Crime Manor" Miss Marple added to the conversation. And once more, there was a nod of assertion throughout the room. Hound badgered around, picking up books and exclaiming "Aha!" and "Eureka!", his absurdist genre was reaching the point of utter farce.

"She had it coming" Spade said, looking down at the body, taking a long drawl from his cigarette.

And for once in her entire career, Miss Jane Marple found that she truly did not care how the victim was murdered.

… It was probably the butler, anyway.

AFTERWORD

Paul Ellis

———

ARNA touched me this time last year when its' then editors Callie Henderson and Nancy Lee published two A5 pages of me whining about my own unoriginality. When I found out that the Publications Director position in SASS was up for grabs, I ran knowing that at least part of me wanted this for reasons other than the fact it would stand out on my significantly bare CV. After working on the journal for several months, I discovered that writing is much more straightforward than editing and that I had been lying to myself. It was all about the CV.

Thank heavens for Julian Larnach. I know you'll read this next line in the afterword of most ARNA's, but this time it really is true. Without Julian, there would be no ARNA 2010. He drove this project from the get-go, doing what was required of him as co-Editor in Chief tremendously and then a lot of my job enthusiastically as well. Thanks also goes to all of our sub-editors, our (In)Designer Alistair Stephenson and everyone in SASS and elsewhere that helped put this together, especially our writers.

While editing was much more difficult than I expected, I am proud that I have helped at least in part to produce this journal. ARNA is remarkable. I know for a fact that being published in it will make you forget for anywhere up to two weeks that your Arts degree is fruitless and you'll never have a career. In all seriousness though, ARNA is a great showcase for Arts students. If you take one thing from this publication, I hope it is this. Every Arts student is an artist, whether they realise it or not. Even the essays they're forced to write, without even mentioning the other wonderful things we've seen them produce for this journal, are beautiful.

———

www.ingramcontent.com/pod-product-compliance
Lightning Source LLC
Chambersburg PA
CBHW071441260626
47170CB00008B/2787